HAR

||||| barcode ||||| 10678254

Russian phrasebook

Alexandra Borodulina

Rachel Farmer

McGraw·Hill

New York   Chicago   San Francisco   Lisbon   London   Madrid   Mexico City
Milan   New Delhi   San Juan   Seoul   Singapore   Sydney   Toronto

The McGraw·Hill Companies

ISBN 0-07-148250-4

Editor & Project Manager
Anna Stevenson

Publishing Manager
Patrick White

Prepress
Isla MacLean
Nadia Cornuau

CONTENTS

INTRODUCTION

This brand new English-Russian phrasebook from Harrap is ideal for anyone wishing to try out their foreign language skills while travelling abroad. The information is practical and clearly presented, helping you to overcome the language barrier and mix with the locals.

Each section features a list of useful words and a selection of common phrases: some of these you will read or hear, while others will help you to express yourself. The simple phonetic transcription system, specifically designed for English speakers, ensures that you will always make yourself understood.

The book also includes a mini bilingual dictionary of around 4,000 words, so that more adventurous users can build on the basic structures and engage in more complex conversations.

Concise information on local culture and customs is provided, along with practical tips to save you time. After all, you're on holiday – time to relax and enjoy yourself! There is also a food and drink glossary to help you make sense of menus, and ensure that you don't miss out on any of the national or regional specialities.

Remember that any effort you make will be appreciated. So don't be shy – have a go!

PRONUNCIATION AND ALPHABET

Pronunciation

English speakers can generally pronounce Russian sounds without too much difficulty and reading Russian is easier than reading English as the spelling is largely phonetic. In this book you will find most Russian phrases transliterated into English phonetic spelling to make things easier for you.

If a word has more than one syllable, one vowel will be pronounced more strongly than the others. Where a vowel appears in bold print, say it with more emphasis. If you put the emphasis on the wrong syllable, you might change the meaning of the word.

Vowels are pronounced separately from each other, except for the combinations ye, yo, yoo, ya, oï, aï, yeï. So, for example, **Rasiya** (Russia) is pronounced *ras-i-ya*.

Alphabet

letter	name of letter	pronunciation	transcription
А а	a	a as in f**a**ther	a
Б б	beh	b	b
В в	veh	v	v
Г г	geh	g as in **g**ood	g
Д д	deh	d	d
Е е	yeh	ye as in **ye**s	ye
Ё ё	yoh	yo as in **yo**ghurt	yo
Ж ж	zhes	zh as in plea**s**ure	zh
З з	zeh	z as in **z**oo	z
И и	ee	ee as in str**ee**t	i
Й й	ee kr**a**tkaye	short ee sound as in to**y**	ï
К к	ka	k	k
Л л	el	l	l
М м	em	m	m
Н н	en	n	n
О о	o	o as in b**o**rn	o

letter	name of letter	pronunciation	transcription
П п	peh	p	p
Р р	er	r	r
С с	es	s	s
Т т	teh	t	t
У у	oo	oo as in b**oo**t	oo
Ф ф	ef	f	f
Х х	kha	ch as in lo**ch**	H
Ц ц	tse	ts as in ca**ts**	ts
Ч ч	cheh	ch as in **ch**icken	ch
Ш ш	sha	sh as in **sh**ip	sh
Щ щ	shia	shsh as in Spani**sh sh**erry	sch
ъ	tv**o**rdy znak	a rarely used letter which makes a tiny gap between syllables	'
ы	iy	i as in **i**ll (pronounced with the tongue drawn back and the lips slightly apart)	y
ь	my**a**Hki znak	softens the previous consonant, as if adding a soft **y** sound to it	'
Э э	eh	e as in l**e**g	e
Ю ю	yoo	u as in **u**niverse	yoo
Я я	ya	ya as in **ya**k	ya

ABBREVIATIONS USED IN THIS BOOK

acc.	accusative	*n*	neuter
adj	adjective	*nom.*	nominative
adv	adverb	*pl*	plural
dat.	dative	*prep*	preposition; prepositional
f	feminine		
gen.	genitive	*sg*	singular
instr.	instrumental	*v*	verb
m	masculine		

EVERYDAY CONVERSATION

(i)

Russians have three names: a first name *(imya)*, a patronymic name *(ochistva)*, derived from the father's first name, and a family name *(familiya)*. When speaking to acquaintances or work colleagues, people address each other using the formal word for you *(vy)* and use the person's first name followed by their patronymic name, which changes depending on whether they are male or female. For example, if a man is called Ivan and his father Baris, he will be called Ivan Barisavich; if a woman is called Natalya and her father Ivan, she will be called Natalya Ivanovna. You should also use *vy* when speaking to more than one person.

When speaking to a friend or family member, people address each other using the informal word for you *(ty)* and tend to use just the person's first name or a diminutive of it. The Russians love diminutives and will use these in informal relationships. A single name can generate several different diminutives. For example, Aliksandr (Alexander) can be shortened to Sasha, Sashen'ka, Sachoolya, Shoora etc.

When approaching a stranger, you should say *dyevooshka* for a young woman and *maladoï chilavyek* for a young man, or you can just say *skazhyti, pazhaloosta* (tell me, please).

People only kiss each other on the cheek on special occasions, for example when meeting after a long separation.

The basics

bye	пока *paka*, до встречи *da fstryechi*
excuse me	извините *izviniti*
good afternoon	добрый день *dobry dyen'*
goodbye	до свидания *da svidaniya*
good evening	добрый вечер *dobry vyechir*
good morning	доброе утро *dobraye ootra*

goodnight	спокойной ночи *spakoïnaï nochi*
hello	*(when using "ty")* здравствуй *zdrastvooï*; *(when using "vy")* здравствуйте *zdrastvooïtye*
hi	привет *privyet*
no	нет *nyet*
OK	хорошо *Harasho*
pardon	простите *prastiti*
please	пожалуйста *pazhaloosta*
thanks, thank you	спасибо *spasiba*
yes	да *da*

Expressing yourself

I'd like ...
я бы хотел *(m)*/хотела *(f)* ...
ya by Hatyel/Hatyela ...

we'd like ...
мы бы хотели ...
my by Hatyeli ...

do you want ...?
вы хотите ...?
vy Hatiti ...?

do you have ...?
у вас есть ...?
oo vas yes't' ...?

is there a ...?
здесь есть ...?
z'dyes' yes't' ...?

are there any ...?
здесь есть ...?
z'dyes' yes't' ...?

how ...?
как ...?
kak ...?

why ...?
почему ...?
pachimoo ...?

when ...?
когда ...?
kagda ...?

what ...?
что ...?
shto ...?

where is ... ?
где ... ?
gdye ...?

where are ...?
где ...?
gdye ...?

how much is it?
сколько это стоит?
skol'ka eta stoit?

what is it?
что это?
shto eta?

do you speak English?
вы говорите по-английски?
vy gavariti pa-angliski?

where are the toilets, please?
вы не подскажите, где здесь туалет?
vy ni patskazhyti, gdye z'dyes' tooalyet?

how are you?
как ваши дела?
kak vashy dila?

fine, thanks
спасибо, хорошо
spasiba, Harasho

thanks very much
большое спасибо
bal'shoye spasiba

no, thanks
нет, спасибо
nyet, spasiba

yes, please
да, если можно
da, yesli mozhna

you're welcome
пожалуйста
pazhaloosta

I'm sorry
мне очень жаль
mnye ochin' zhal'

see you later
ещё увидимся
ischyo oovidimsya

Understanding

внимание	attention
нельзя …	do not …
вход	entrance
добро пожаловать	welcome
выход	exit
от себя	push
к себе	pull
бесплатно	free
парковка запрещена	no parking
не курить	no smoking
открыто	open
закрыто	closed
не работает	out of order
зарезервирован	reserved
туалеты	toilets

есть
yes't'
there's/there are …

вы не против, если …
vy ni protif, yesli?
do you mind if …?

одну минуточку
adnoo minootachkoo
one moment, please

присаживайтесь, пожалуйста
prisazhyvaitis' pazhaloosta
please take a seat

PROBLEMS UNDERSTANDING RUSSIAN

Expressing yourself

pardon?
простите?
prastiti ?

what?
что-что?
shto-shto?

could you repeat that, please?
вы не могли бы повторить, пожалуйста?
vy ni magli by paftarit', pazhaloosta?

could you speak more slowly?
вы не могли бы говорить медленнее?
vy ni magli by gavarit' medliniye?

I don't understand
я не понимаю
ya ni panimayoo

I only understand a little Russian
я плохо понимаю по-русски
ya ploHa panimayoo pa-rooski

I can understand Russian but I can't speak it
я понимаю по-русски, но не говорю
ya panimayoo pa-rooski, no ni gavaryoo

I hardly speak any Russian
я почти не говорю по-русски
ya pachti ni gavaryoo pa-rooski

do you speak English?
вы говорите по-английски?
vy gavariti pa-angliski?

how do you say … in Russian?
как будет … по-русски?
kak boodit … pa-rooski?

what's that called in Russian?
как это называется по-русски?
kak eta nazyvaitsa pa-rooski?

how do you spell "street" in Russian?
как пишется "street" по-русски?
kak pishetsa "street" pa-rooski?

could you write it down for me?
вы можете мне это написать?
vy mozhyti mnye eta napisat'?

Understanding

вы понимаете?
vy panimaiti?
do you understand?

это значит …
eta znachit …
it means …

я вам напишу
ya vam napishoo
I'll write it down for you

это что-то вроде …
eta shto-ta vrodi …
it's a kind of …

SPEAKING ABOUT THE LANGUAGE

Expressing yourself

I learned a few words from my phrasebook
я выучил несколько слов из разговорника
ya vyoochil nyeskal'ka slof iz razgavornika

I did it at school but I've forgotten everything
я учил *(m)*/учила *(f)* его в школе, но всё уже забыл *(m)*/забыла *(f)*
ya oochil/oochila ivo f shkolye, no fsyo oozhe zabyl/zabyla

I can just about get by
я могу выйти из положения
ya magoo vyïti is palazheniya

I hardly know two words!
я и двух слов не знаю!
ya i dvooH slof ni znayoo!

I find Russian a difficult language
я думаю, что русский – очень сложный язык
ya doomayoo, shto rooski – ochin' slozhny yazyk

I know the basics but no more than that
я знаю самые простые вещи, не более того
ya znayoo samyye prastyye vyeschi, ni boliye tavo

people speak too quickly for me
люди говорят слишком быстро для меня
lyoodi gavaryat slishkam bystra dlya minya

Understanding

у вас хорошее произношение
oo vas Haroshyye praiznasheniye
you have a good accent

вы хорошо говорите по-русски
vy Harasho gavariti pa-rooski
you speak good Russian

ASKING THE WAY

EVERYDAY CONVERSATION

Expressing yourself

excuse me, can you tell me where the … is, please?
извините, вы не подскажите, где находится …?
izviniti, vy ni patskazhyti, gdye naHoditsa …?

which way is it to … ?
как мне пройти к …?
kak mnye praïti k …?

is there a … near here?
здесь рядом есть …?
z'dyes' ryadam yes't' …?

can you tell me how to get to … ?
вы не подскажите, как мне добраться до …?
vy ni patskazhyti, kak mnye dabratsa da …?

could you show me on the map?
покажите мне, пожалуйста, на карте?
pakazhyti mnye, pazhaloosta, na karti?

is there a map of the town somewhere?
где можно найти план города?
gdye mozhna naïti plan gorada?

is it far?
это далеко?
eta daliko?

can I go on foot?
я могу дойти пешком?
ya magoo daïti pishkom?

I'm looking for …
я ищу …
ya ischyoo …

I'm lost
я заблудился *(m)*/заблудилась *(f)*
ya zabloodilsya/zabloodilas'

what is the name of this street/square?
как называется эта улица/площадь?
kak nazyvaitsa eta oolitsa/ploschit'?

Understanding

идите прямо	go straight ahead
идите вниз по улице	go down
идите вверх по улице	go up
не сворачивайте	keep going
налево	left
направо	right
поверните	turn

вы пешком?
vy pishkom?
are you on foot?

вам лучше взять такси
vam lootshe vzyat' taksi
you'd better go by taxi

это в пяти минут ходьбы
eta f piti minootaH Had'by
it's five minutes on foot

здесь на машине пять минут
z'dyes' na mashyni pyat' minoot
it's five minutes away by car

это первый/второй/третий поворот направо
eta pyervy/fftaroi/tryeti pavarot naprava
it's the first/second/third on the right

идите в этом направлении
iditi v etam napravlyenii
go in this direction

поверните направо на перекрестке с круговым движением
pavirniti naprava na pirikryostki s kroogavym dvizheniyem
turn right at the roundabout

у банка поверните налево
oo banka paviriniti nalyeva
turn left at the bank

вам в следующий выход
vam f slyedooschi vyHat
take the next exit

там будет указатель
tam boodit ookazatil'
there will be a sign

это сразу за углом
eta srazoo za ooglom
it's just round the corner

это недалеко
eta nidaliko
it's not far

GETTING TO KNOW PEOPLE

The basics

bad	плохой *plaHoï*
beautiful	красивый *krasivy*
boring	скучный *skooshny*
cheap	дешёвый *dishovy*
expensive	дорогой *daragoï*
good	хороший *Haroshy*
great	замечательный *zamichyatil'ny*
interesting	интересный *intiryesny*
nice	мило *mila*
not bad	неплохо *niploHa*
well	хорошо *Harasho*
to hate	ненавидеть *ninavidit'*
to like	нравиться *nravitsa*
to love	любить *lyoobit'*

INTRODUCING YOURSELF AND FINDING OUT ABOUT OTHER PEOPLE

Expressing yourself

my name's ...
меня зовут ...
minya zavoot ...

what's your name?
как вас зовут?
kak vas zavoot?

pleased to meet you!
очень приятно познакомиться!
ochin' priyatna paznakomitsa!

me too
взаимно
vzaimna

this is my husband/my wife
это мой муж/моя жена
eta moï moosh/maya zhynaeta

this is my partner, Karen
это моя подруга, Карен
eta maya padrooga, karin

I'm English
я из Англии
ya iz anglii

where are you from?
а вы откуда?
a vy atkooda?

how old are you?
сколько вам лет?
skol'ka vam lyet?

what do you do for a living?
чем вы занимаетесь?
chyem vy zanimaityes'?

I work
я работаю
ya rabotayoo

I'm a teacher
я учитель
ya oochityel'

I work part-time
я работаю на полставки
ya rabotayoo na polstafki

I'm retired
я на пенсии
ya na pyensii

I have two children
у меня двое детей
oo minya dvoye dityeï

two boys and a girl
два мальчика и девочка
dva mal'chika i dyevachka

we're Welsh
мы из Уэльса
my iz ooel'sa

I'm from …
я из …
ya iz …

I'm 22
мне двадцать два
mnye dvatsat' lyet

are you a student?
вы студент/студентка?
vy stoodyent/stoodyentka?

I'm studying law
я изучаю право
ya izoochayoo prava

I stay at home with the children
я сижу дома, воспитываю детей
ya sizhoo doma, vaspityvayoo dityeï

I work in marketing
я занимаюсь маркетингом
ya zanimayoos' marketingam

I'm self-employed
у меня своё дело
oo minya svayo dyela

we don't have any children
у нас нет детей
oo nas nyet dityeï

a boy of five and a girl of two
сыну пять лет, а дочке два года
synoo pyat' lyet, a dochkye dva goda

have you ever been to Britain?
вы были когда-нибудь в Англии?
vy byli kagda-niboot' v anglii?

Understanding

вы англичанин *(m)*/**англичанка** *(f)*?
vy anglichanin/anglichanka?
are you English?

я неплохо знаю Англию
ya niploHa znayoo angliyoo
I know England quite well

мне бы хотелось когда-нибудь съездить в Шотландию
mnye by Hatyelas' kagda-niboot' s-yez'dit' v shatlandiyoo
I'd love to go to Scotland one day

мы тоже здесь на отдыхе
my tozhe z'dyes' na atdyHe
we're on holiday here too

TALKING ABOUT YOUR STAY

Expressing yourself

I'm here on business
я здесь по работе
ya z'dyes' pa raboti

I arrived three days ago
я приехал *(m)*/**приехала** *(f)* **три дня назад**
ya priyeHal/priyeHala tri dnya nazat

we've been here for a week
мы здесь уже неделю
my z'dyes' oozhe nidyelyoo

I'm only here for a weekend
мы приехали только на выходные
my priyeHali tol'ka na vyHadnyye

this is our first time in Russia
мы первый раз в России
my pyervy ras v rasii

we're on holiday
у нас отпуск/каникулы
oo nas otpoosk/kanikooly

we're just passing through
мы здесь проездом
my z'dyes' prayezdam

we're on our honeymoon
у нас медовый месяц
oo nas midovy myesits

we're here to celebrate our wedding anniversary
мы отмечаем годовщину свадьбы
my atmichyaim gadafschinoo svad'by

we're here with friends
мы здесь с друзьями
my z'dyes' z drooz'yami

we're touring around
мы осматриваем окрестности
my asmatrivaim akryesnas'ti

we've been recommended to visit ...
нам посоветовали побывать в ...
nam pasavyetavali pabyvat' v ...

Understanding

желаем хорошо провести время!
zhylaim Harasho pravisti vryemya
enjoy your stay!

вы первый раз в России?
vy pyervy ras v rasii?
is this your first time in Russia?

вы давно приехали?
vy davno priyeHali?
did you arrive long ago?

вы надолго приехали?
vy nadolga priyeHali?
are you staying long?

вам здесь нравиться?
vam z'dyes' nravitsa?
do you like it here?

вы были в ...?
vy byli v ...?
have you been to ...?

STAYING IN TOUCH

Expressing yourself

we should stay in touch
надо будет продолжить общение в будущем
nada boodit pradolzhyt' apschyeniye v boodooschyem

I'll give you my e-mail address
запишите мой e-mail
zapishyti moï i-meil

here's my address, if ever you come to Britain
вот мой адрес, если вы когда-нибудь соберётесь в Англию
vot moï adris, yesli vy kagda-niboot' sabiryotis' v angliyoo

Understanding

вы дадите мне свой адрес/телефон?
vy dadíti mnye svoï adris/tilifon?
will you give me your address/phone number?

у вас есть e-mail?
oo vas yes't' i-meil?
do you have an e-mail address?

приезжайте, мы всегда рады вас видеть
priizhaïti, my vsigda rady vas vidit'
come and visit, we're always happy to see you

EXPRESSING YOUR OPINION

> **Some informal expressions**
>
> **такая скукотища** what a bore
> **там такая тоска** it's such a drag there
> **это было просто супер/потрясно** it was totally brilliant
> **мы повеселились/оторвались на славу** we had a fantastic time

Expressing yourself

I really like ...
мне действительно нравиться ...
mnye distvitil'na nravitsa ...

I really liked ...
мне действительно понравилось ...
mnye distvitil'na panravilas' ...

I don't like ...
я не люблю ...
ya ni lyooblyoo ...

I didn't like ...
мне не понравилось ...
mnye ni panravilas' ...

I love ...
я люблю ...
ya lyooblyoo ...

I loved ...
мне очень понравилось ...
mnye ochin' panravilas' ...

I would like …
я бы хотел/хотела …
ya by Hatyel/Hulyela …

I find it …
мне кажется, что …
mnye kazhytsa, shto …

I found it …
мне показалось, что …
mnye pakazalas', shto …

it's lovely
это чудесно
eta chyoodyesna

it was lovely
это было чудесно
eta byla chyoodyesna

I agree
согласен *(m)*/согласна *(f)*
ya saglasin/saglasna

I don't agree
я не согласен *(m)*/не согласна *(f)*
ya ni saglasin/saglasna

I don't know
я не знаю
ya ni znayoo

I don't mind
я не против
ya ni protif

it sounds interesting
это интересная идея
eta intiryesnaya idyeya

I don't like the sound of it
мне совсем не по душе эта идея
mnye safsyem ni pa dooshe eta idyeya

it really annoys me
это действует мне на нервы
eta dyeïstvooyet mnye na nervy

it was boring
было скучно
byla skooshna

it's too busy
там очень шумно
tam ochin' shoomna

it's very quiet
это очень спокойное место
eta ochin' spakoïnaya myesta

it gets very busy in the evening
ближе к вечеру там собирается много народу
blizhe k vyechiroo tam sabiraitsa mnoga narodoo

we had a great time
мы чудесно провели время
my choodyesna pravili vryemya

there was a really good atmosphere
там была очень располагающая атмосфера
tam byla ochin' raspalagayooschiya atmasfyera

we met some nice people
мы познакомились с приятными людьми
my paznakomilis' s priyatnymi lyood'mi

we found a great hotel
мы нашли превосходную гостиницу
my nashli privasHodnooyoo gastinitsoo

Understanding

вы любите ...?
vy lyoobiti?
do you like ...?

вы хорошо провели время?
vy Harasho pravili vryemya?
did you enjoy yourselves?

вам нужно побывать в ...
vam noozhna pabyvat' v ...
you should go to ...

вам там понравится
vam tam panravitsa
you'll like it there

я бы посоветовал *(m)*/**посоветовала** *(f)* **...**
ya by pasavyetyval/pasavyetyvala ...
I recommend ...

это чудесное место
eta chyoodnaye myesta
it's a lovely area

там не так много туристов
tam ni tak mnogo tooristaf
there aren't too many tourists there

не ездите в выходные, там слишком много народу
ni yez'diti v vyHadnyi, tam slishkam mnoga narodoo
don't go at the weekend, it's too busy

TALKING ABOUT THE WEATHER

Expressing yourself

have you heard the weather forecast for tomorrow?
вы слышали прогноз погоды на завтра?
vy slyshali pragnos pagody na zaftra?

what's the temperature today?
какая сегодня температура?
kakaya sivodnya timpiratoora?

it's going to be nice
обещают хорошую погоду
abischyayoot Haroshooyoo pagodoo

it isn't going to be nice
обещают плохую погоду
abischyayoot plaHooyoo pagodoo

it's really hot
очень жарко
ochin' zharka

it gets very cold at night
ночи очень холодные
nochi ochin' Halodnyye

there are frosts at night
по ночам бывают заморозки
pa nachyam byvayoot zamaraski

it's very humid here
здесь высокая влажность
z'dyes' vysokaya vlazhnast'

there was a thunderstorm
была гроза
byla graza

it rained/snowed a few times
несколько раз шёл дождь/снег
nyeskal'ka ras shol dosht'/snyek

the weather has been beautiful all week
всю неделю стояла чудесная погода
fsyoo nidyelyoo stayala chyoodyesnaya pagoda

we've been lucky with the weather
нам повезло с погодой
nam pavizlo s pagodai

Understanding

собирается дождь
sabiraitsa dosht'
it's supposed to rain

завтра похолодает/потеплеет
zaftra paHaladait/ patiplyeit
tomorrow it'll get colder/warmer

обещали хорошую погоду до конца недели
abischali Haroshooyoo pagodoo da kantsa nidyeli
they've forecast good weather for the rest of the week

завтра будет так же жарко/холодно/ветрено/дождливо
zaftra boodit tag zhe zharka/Holadna/vyetrina/dazhdliva
it will be hot/cold/windy/rainy again tomorrow

Some informal expressions

такая холодина! it's freezing!
у меня зуб на зуб не попадает my teeth are chattering
льет как из ведра it's bucketing down

TRAVELLING

The basics

airport	аэропорт *airaport*
boarding	посадка *pasatka*
boarding card	посадочный талон *pasadachny talon*
boat	теплоход *tiplaHot*
bus	автобус *aftoboos*
bus station	автовокзал *aftavagzal*
bus stop	автобусная остановка *aftoboosnaya astanofka*
car	машина *mashyna*
check-in	регистрация *rigistratsyya*
coach	автобус *aftoboos*
ferry	паром *parom*
flight	рейс *ryeïs*
gate	выход *vyHat*
left-luggage (office)	камера хранения *kamira Hranyeniya*
local train	электричка *iliktrichka*
luggage	багаж *bagash*
map	карта *karta*
motorway	автострада *aftastrada*
passport	паспорт *paspart*
plane	самолёт *samalyot*
platform	платформа *platforma*
railway station	вокзал *vagzal*
return (ticket)	билет в оба конца *bilyet v oba kantsa*, туда обратно *tooda abratna*
road	дорога *daroga*
shuttle bus	пригородный автобус *prigaradny aftoboos*
single (ticket)	билет в один конец *bilyet v adin kanyets*
street	улица *oolitsa*
streetmap	план города *plan gorada*
taxi	такси *taksi*
terminal	терминал *tyerminal*
ticket	билет *bilyet*
timetable	расписание *raspisaniye*
town centre	центр города *tsentr gorada*

train	поезд *poist*
tram	трамвай *tramvaï*
trolleybus	троллейбус *tralyeïboos*
underground	метро *myitro*
underground station	станция метро *stantsyya myitro*
to book	бронировать/забронировать *braniravat'/ zabraniravat'*
to hire	брать в прокат *brat' f prakat*

Expressing yourself

where can I buy tickets?
где можно купить билеты?
gdye mozhna koopit' bilyety?

a ticket to ..., please
билет до ..., пожалуйста
bilyet da ..., pazhaloosta

I'd like to book a ticket
я хочу забронировать билет
ya Hachyoo zabraniravat' bilyet

how much is a ticket to ...?
сколько стоит билет до ...?
skol'ka stoit bilyet da ...?

are there any concessions for students?
есть ли скидки для студентов?
yes't' li skitki dlya stoodyentaf?

could I have a timetable, please?
у вас есть расписание?
oo vas yes't' raspisaniye?

is there a later plane/train/bus?
когда отправляется следующий самолёт/поезд/автобус?
kagda atpravlyaitsa slyedooschi samalyot/poist/aftoboos?

how long does the journey take?
сколько времени длится поездка?
skol'ka vryemini dlitsa poestka?

could you call the porter, please?
позовите, пожалуйста, носильщика
pazaviti, pazhaloosta, nasil'schika

here is my ticket
вот мой билет
vot moï bilyet

is this seat free?
это место свободно?
eta myesta svabodna?

I'm sorry, there's someone sitting there
извините, это место занято
izviniti, eta myesta zanyata

Understanding

Making sense of abbreviations

A = автобус bus
M = метро metro
TM = трамвай tram
Tp = троллейбус trolley bus

прибытие	arrivals
отменён	cancelled
переход	connection
отправление	departures
вход	entrance
входа нет	no entry
справочное бюро	information
задерживается	delayed
выход	exit
туалеты	toilets
М (мужской туалет)	gents
Ж (женский туалет)	ladies
билеты	tickets
бюро находок	lost property office
маршрутка	minibus fixed-route taxi

все билеты проданы
fsye bilyety prodany
everything is fully booked

BY PLANE

(i)

Domestic flights are operated by several Russian airlines, including Aeroflot, Transaero and Siberian Airlines. Because air travel has become so expensive for Russians in recent years, there are fewer domestic flights than there used to be. However, you can still fly between the major cities and there are frequent and regular flights between Saint Petersburg and Moscow.

You can make reservations in travel agents, which you will find in all the big cities. Staff usually speak English.

Expressing yourself

where is the British Airways check-in?
где регистрация на рейс компании British Airways?
gdye rigistratsyya na ryeïs kampanii british airways?

these items go as my luggage
эти вещи я сдаю в багаж
eti vyeschi ya zdayoo v bagash

I'll take this bag as hand luggage
эту сумку я беру с собой в салон
etoo soomkoo ya biroo s saboï f salon

what is the charge for overweight baggage?
сколько стоит перевес багажа?
skol'ka stoit pirivyes bagazha?

what time is flight … boarding?
во сколько начинается посадка на рейс …?
va skol'ka nachinaitsa pasatka na ryeïs …?

I'd like to confirm my return flight
я хочу подтвердить дату возврата
ya Hachoo patvirdit' datoo vazvrata

I can't find my luggage
я не могу найти свой багаж
ya ni magoo naïti svoï bagash

one of my suitcases is missing
пропал один из моих чемоданов
prapal adin iz maiH chimadanaf

I want to report the loss of my luggage
я хочу заявить о пропаже багажа
ya Hachoo zayavit' a prapazhe bagazha

I've left something on the plane
я кое-что забыл *(m)*/забыла *(f)* в самолёте
ya koye-shto zabyl/zabyla f samalyoti

the plane was two hours late
самолёт опоздал на два часа
samalyot apazdal na dva chisa

no one met me
меня не встретили
minya ni fstryetili

I've missed my connection
я не успел *(m)*/не успела *(f)* на пересадку
ya ni oospyel/ni oospyela na pirisatkoo

Understanding

прилет	arrivals
вылет	departure
камера хранения	left luggage
выдача багажа	baggage reclaim
камера невостребованных вещей	lost property
регистрация	check-in
таможня	customs
зал ожидания	departure lounge
международные авиалинии	international airlines
внутренние авиалинии	domestic flights
магазин "duty free"	duty free shop
декларирование багажа/ «красный» коридор	goods to declare/red corridor
срочная посадка	immediate boarding
«зеленый» коридор	green corridor (nothing to declare)
паспортный контроль	passport control
бронирование и оформление билетов	booking desk
медицинская помощь	first aid

покажите, пожалуйста, ваш паспорт
pakazhyti, pazhaloosta, vash paspart
could I have your passport, please?

пожалуйста, подождите в зале ожидания
vpazhaloosta, padazhditi v zali azhydaniya
please wait in the departure lounge

вам место у окна или в проходе?
vam myesta oo akna ili f praHodi?
would you like a window seat or an aisle seat?

будет пересадка в …
boodit pirisatka v …
you'll have to change in …

сколько у вас единиц багажа?
skol'ka oo vas yidinits bagazha?
how many bags do you have?

откройте, пожалуйста, ваш чемодан
atkroiti, pazhaloosta, vash chimadan
could you please open your suitcase?

положите все ваши вещи сюда
palazhyti fsye vashi vyeschi syooda
put all your luggage here

вы сами упаковывали вещи?
vy sami oopakovyvali vyeschi?
did you pack all your bags yourself?

у вас перевес пять килограмм
oo vas pirivyes pyat' kilagram
your luggage is five kilos overweight

вот ваш посадочный талон
vot vash pasadachny talon
here's your boarding card

посадка начнется в …
pasatka nachnyotsa v …
boarding will begin at …

пожалуйста, пройдите к выходу номер …
pazhaloosta, praiditi k vyHadoo nomir …
please proceed to gate number …

заканчивается посадка на рейс …
zakanchivaitsa pasatka na ryeïs …
this is a final call for …

по этому телефону вы сможете узнать, прибыл ли ваш багаж
pa etamoo tilifonoo vy smozhyti ooznat', pribyl li vash bagash
you can call this number to check if your luggage has arrived

BY TRAIN, COACH, BUS, UNDERGROUND, TRAM

(i)

Russian trains are slow but generally quite comfortable. You can buy tickets at stations or specialized agencies, **касса предварительной продажи** (*kasa pryidvarityel'naï pradazhy*), for travel on the same day or several days ahead (up to 45 days before you want to travel). On the main lines, trains are divided into four categories. **Мягкие вагоны** (*myaHkyei vagony*) have two-seater compartments, which are quite spacious and the equivalent of travelling first class. **Купейные вагоны** (*koopyeïnyye vagony*) are slightly cheaper, and have compartments with four bunks – they are the most popular. **Плацкартные вагоны** (*platskartnyye vagony*) have bunks all down the aisle. **Общие вагоны** (*opschiye vagony*) have only basic bunks, with no mattresses or sheets. Trains usually have a restaurant car. Suburban trains are called **электрички** (*iliktrichki*).

In Saint Petersburg and Moscow, the quickest and simplest way to get around is by metro (trains run every two minutes). In Moscow, some of the stations are extremely visually impressive, decorated with marble, paintings and elaborate chandeliers. Trains run from 6am to 1am. In Moscow, you can buy swipe cards **магнитные карточки** (*magnitnyye kartachki*) giving you access to the stations and allowing you to travel on the whole network. Monthly cards **единые билеты** (*yedinyye bilyety*) for all types of public transport are sold at metro stations and kiosks.

Russian towns usually have decent bus and tram services, but they are less regular than the metro and the vehicles are often dilapidated. You can buy tickets **проездные билеты** (*praiznyi bilyety*) on the bus or from newpaper kiosks. When you get on, you must stamp your ticket in one of the machines above the seats or give it to the conductor.

Expressing yourself

where can I get a map of the underground?
где можно взять схему метрополитена?
gdye mozhna vzyat' sHyemoo myetrapalitena?

how do I get to ...?
как мне доехать до ...?
kak mnye dayeHat' da ...?

what time is the next train to ...?
когда следующий поезд до ...?
kagda slyedooschi poist da ...?

what time is the last train?
во сколько уходит последний поезд?
va skol'ka ooHodit paslyedni poist?

which platform is it for the train to ...?
с какой платформы отправляется поезд до ...?
s kakoï platformy atpravlyaitsa poist da ...?

which platform is it for the train from ...?
на какую платформу прибывает поезд из ...?
na kakooyoo platformoo pribyvait poist iz ...?

where can I catch a bus to ...?
на каком автобусе я доеду до ...?
na kakom aftoboosi ya dayedoo da ...?

which line do I take to get to ...?
на какой ветке находится станция ...?
na kakoï vyetki naHoditsa stantsyya ...?

where do I have to change?
где мне лучше сделать пересадку?
gdye mnye lootshe z'dyelat' pirisatkoo?

where is the underground station here?
где находится ближайшая станция метро?
gdye naHoditsa blizhaïshaya stantsyya mitro?

is this where the coach leaves for ...?
отсюда уходит автобус на/до ...?
atsyooda ooHodit aftoboos na/da ...?

can you tell me when I need to get off?
вы не подскажете, когда мне выходить?
vy ni patskazhyti, kagda mnye vyHadit'?

excuse me, does this bus go to ...?
простите, этот автобус идёт до ...?
pras'titi, etat aftoboos idyot da ...?

I've missed my train/bus
я пропустил свой поезд/автобус
ya prapoos'til svoï poist/aftoboos

please stop at the next stop
остановите, пожалуйста, на следующей
astanaviti, pazhaloosta, na slyedooschyïi

Understanding

к поездам до станций	to the trains
к пригородным поездам	to the local trains
к поездам дальнего следования	to the long distance trains
зал ожидания	departure lounge
касса	ticket office
пригородные кассы	suburban ticket office
предварительная продажа билетов	advance bookings
администратор	administrator
выход в город	exit to the town
посадки нет	no boarding
к платформе №	to platform no
путь №	line no

остановка вон там, справа/за углом/через дорогу
astanofka von tam, sprava/za ooglom/chiris darogoo
there's a stop over there on the right/around the corner/across the road

желательно без сдачи
zhylatil'na biz zdachi
exact money only, please

вам билет в купе или плацкарт?
vam bilyet v koope ili platskart?
would you like a ticket for a compartment or an open carriage?

вам нужно будет сделать пересадку на …
vam noozhna boodit z'dyelat' pirisatkoo na …
you'll have to change at …

вам нужно сесть на автобус номер …
vam noozhna syes't' na aftoboos nomir…
you need to get the number … bus

ваш билет, пожалуйста
vash bilyet, pazhaloosta
your ticket, please

этот поезд останавливается в …
etat poist astanavlivaitsa v …
this train calls at …

через две остановки
chiriz dvye astanofki
two stops from here

вам выходить на следующей
vam vyHadit' na slyedooschi
yours is the next stop

BY CAR

Given the bad condition of the roads and the poor signposting, it's best to avoid driving in Russia. If you do want to hire a car when you are there, you will need to be at least 21 and hold an international driving licence. Seatbelts must be worn in the front and speed limits are 60km/h in towns and 90km/h on open roads. Be aware that the traffic police **ГАИ** (GAI) have a strong presence. There are few service stations outside larger cities. It's best to park near big hotels as car theft and removal of parts are all too common.

Taxis are available for hire when the green light is showing. It's best to negotiate the price of your trip before you set off as meters are rare and several factors can affect prices. In the evening and late at night fares are higher than during the day, and they are often doubled for foreigners. There is no extra charge for luggage.

Маршрутные такси *(marshrootnyye taksi)* are minibuses which follow a fixed route and can seat about ten people. They are faster than buses and much cheaper than taxis. It is also often possible to hitch a lift with locals looking to make a bit of extra money, but you will have to negotiate a price. Note, however, that hitching can be dangerous – if you do choose to travel this way, be vigilant and never accept a lift from a car with more than one person in it.

Expressing yourself

where can I find a service station?
где здесь ближайшая бензоколонка?
gdye z'dyes' blizhaïshaya binzakalonka?

a full tank, please
полный бак, пожалуйста
polny bak, pazhaloosta

I need … litres
мне, пожалуйста, … литров
mnye, pazhaloosta, … litraf

how much is it per litre?
сколько стоит литр?
skol'ka stoit litr?

we got stuck in a traffic jam
мы попали в пробку
my papali f propkoo

excuse me, what is the best way to …?
простите, как мне лучше доехать до …?
pras'titi, kak mnye lootshe dayeHat' da …?

is there a garage near here?
здесь есть поблизости автосервис?
z'dyes' yes't' pablizasti aftasyervis?

can you help us to push the car?
вы не поможете подтолкнуть машину?
vy ni pamozhyti pattalknoot' mashynoo?

the battery's dead
у меня сел аккумулятор
oo minya syel akamoolyatar

I've broken down
у меня сломалась машина
oo minya slamalas' mashyna

we've run out of petrol
у нас кончился бензин
oo nas konchilsya binzin

we've just had an accident
мы только что попали в аварию
my tol'ka shto papali v avariyoo

I've got a puncture and my spare tyre is flat
у меня проколота шина и спущено запасное колесо
oo minya prakolata shyna i spooschina zapasnoye kaliso

I've lost my car keys
я потерял/потеряла ключи от машины
ya patiryal/patiryala klyoochi at mashyny

how long will it take to repair?
сколько времени займёт ремонт?
skol'ka vryemini zaïmyot rimont?

◆ Hiring a car

I'd like to hire a car for a week
я хочу взять машину напрокат на неделю
ya Hachoo vzyat' mashynoo naprakat na nidyelyoo

what's the cost per day?
сколько стоит аренда машины в день?
skol'ka stoit aryenda mashyny v dyen'?

an automatic (car)
машина с автоматической коробкой передач (коробкой-автомат)
mashyna s aftamaticheskaï karopkaï piridach (karopkaï-aftamat)

I'd like to take out comprehensive insurance
я хочу оформить комплексную страховку на машину
ya Hachoo aformit' kompliksnooyu straHovkoo

◆ Getting a taxi

is there a taxi rank near here?
где здесь стоянка такси?
gdye z'dyes' stayanka taksi?

taxi! are you free?
такси! свободно?
taksi! svabodna?

I'd like to go to …
мне нужно в …
mnye noozhna v …

I'd like to book a taxi for 8pm
я хочу заказать такси на восемь вечера
ya Hachoo zakazat' taksi na vosim' vyechira

you can drop me off here, thanks
остановите, пожалуйста, здесь. Спасибо.
astanaviti, pazhaloosta, z'dyes'. Spasiba.

how much will it be to go to the airport?
сколько стоит доехать до аэропорта?
skol'ka stoit dayeHat' da airaporta?

could we please hurry up, I'm going to be late
если можно, побыстрее. я опаздываю
yesli mozhna, pabystryeye. ya apazdyvayoo

how much does the trip cost?
сколько с меня?
skol'ka s minya?

◆ Hitchhiking

I'm going to ...
мне нужно в ...
mnye noozhna v ...

can you drop me off here?
вы можете высадить меня здесь?
vy mozhytye vysadit' minya z'dyes'?

could you take me as far as ...?
вы можете довезти меня до ...?
vy mozhytye davisti minya da ...?

thanks for the lift
спасибо, что подвезли
spasiba, shta padvizli

we hitched a lift
мы поймали попутку
my païmali papootkoo

Understanding

возьмите ваш билет	keep your ticket
аренда автомобилей	car hire
парковка	car park
замедлите ход	slow
парковка запрещена	no parking
стоп	stop
уступи дорогу	give way
объезд	diversion
въезд запрещен	no entry
соблюдайте скоростной режим	observe the speed limit
ДПС	motorway patrol post
ГАИ	traffic police

ваши права, удостоверяющий личность, и кредитную карту, пожалуйста
vashy prava, oodastviryayooschi lichnas't' i kriditnooyoo kartoo, pazhaloosta
I'll need your driving licence, proof of identity and your credit card

вам нужно внести … в качестве залога
vam noozhna vnis'ti … f kachistvi zaloga
you will have to pay … as a deposit

куда подать машину?
kooda padat' mashynoo?
where do I need to drop the car?

куда вам?
kooda vam?
where do you want to go?

хорошо, садитесь, я вас подброшу до …
Harasho, saditis', ya vas padbroshoo da…
alright, get in, I'll take you as far as …

BY BOAT

(i)

Travel agencies offer a variety of cruises on the Volga **Волга** *(vol'ga)*, in particular between Moscow **Москва** *(maskva)* and Saint Petersburg **Санкт Петербург** *(sankt pityerboork)* or to visit ancient cities like **Ярославль** *(yaroslavl')* or **Нижний Новгород** *(nizhni novgarat)*.

Expressing yourself

how long is the crossing?
как долго длится плавание?
kak dolga dlitsa plavaniye?

I'm seasick
меня укачивает
minya ookachivait

Understanding

только для пешеходов	foot passengers only
следующий рейс в …	next crossing at …

ACCOMMODATION

ℹ️

It is essential to book a hotel before you set off, as you will have to give your address when you arrive in Russia in order to obtain a tourist visa. Cheap hotels (around £50–£60 a night) are hard to find. The best hotels are run by western companies and are like 4- or 5-star hotels, ie often very expensive; they will accept credit cards. When you arrive you will have to leave your passport at reception. You will then be given a pass (**пропуск** *propoosk*) to show to the "floor keeper" (**дежурная** *dyizhoornaya*) who will give you your keys.

For a real taste of Russian life, you can stay with a family. Big cities have organizations for this such as the HOFA (Host Families Association) in Saint Petersburg.

There are few youth hostels in Russia.

Foreigners are currently allowed to stay with Russian friends, but they must have received a written invitation and will need to register upon arrival at a local office.

If you want to go camping, you must book at a travel agency before you set off. Campsites are usually open from 1 June to 30 September.

The basics

bath	ванна *vana*
bathroom	ванная комната *vanaya komnata*
bathroom with shower	ванная с душем *vanaya s dooshem*
bed	кровать *kravat'*
bed and breakfast	проживание с завтраком *prazhyvaniye z zaftrakam*
cable television	кабельное телевидение *kabil'naye tilividiniye*
campsite	кемпинг *kyempink*
caravan	фургон *foorgon*

cottage	коттедж *kotedzh*
double bed	двуспальная кровать *dvoospal'naya kravat'*
double room	двухместный номер *dvooHmyestny nomir*
family room	номер на семью *nomir na sim'yoo*
flat	квартира *kvartira*
full-board	полный пансион *polny pansion*
fully inclusive	всё включено *fsyo fklyoochino*
guest	гость *gos't'*
half-board	полупансион *poloopansion*
hotel	гостиница *gastinitsa*
key	ключ *klyooch*
rent	аренда *aryenda*
shower	душ *doosh*
single bed	односпальная кровать *adnaspal'naya kravat'*
single room	одноместный номер *adnamyestny nomir*
tenant	жилец *zhylyets*
tent	палатка *palatka*
toilet	туалет *tooalyet*
youth hostel	турбаза *toorbaza*
to book	бронировать *braniravat'*
to rent	снимать *snimat'*
to reserve	заказывать заранее *zakazyvat' zaraniye*

Expressing yourself

I have a reservation
на моё имя забронирован
na mayo imya zabraniravan

the name's …
моя фамилия …
maya familiya …

do you take credit cards?
вы принимаете кредитные карты?
vy prinimaiti kriditnyi karty?

I'll pay in cash/by credit card
я плачу наличными/кредитной картой
ya plachoo nalichnymi/kriditnaï kartaï

I'll stay for a day/several days/a week
я пробуду здесь сутки/несколько дней/неделю
ya praboodoo z'dyes' sootki/nyeskal'ka dnyeï/nidyelyoo

I'm leaving this evening/tomorrow morning
я уезжаю сегодня вечером/завтра утром
ya ooizhayoo sivodnya vyechiram/zaftra ootram

Understanding

этаж	floor
мест нет	full
регистрация	reception
дежурный администратор	reception staff
туалеты	toilets
свободные места	vacancies

покажите, пожалуйста, ваш паспорт
pakazhyti, pazhaloosta, vash paspart
could I see your passport, please?

заполните, пожалуйста, эту форму
zapolniti, pazhaloosta, etoo formoo
could you fill in this form?

HOTELS

Expressing yourself

do you have any vacancies?
у вас есть свободные номера?
oo vas yes't' svabodnyye namira?

how much is a double room per night?
сколько стоит двухместный номер в сутки?
skol'ka stoit dvooHmyestny nomir f sootki?

I'd like to reserve a double room/a single room
я бы хотел получить одноместный/двухместный номер
ya by Hatyel paloochit' adnamyestny/dvooHmyestny nomir

would it be possible to stay an extra night?
возможно будет остаться еще на ночь?
vazmozhna boodit astatsa ischyo na noch'?

do you have any rooms available for tonight?
есть ли свободные номера на сегодняшний вечер?
yes't' li svabodnyye namira na sivodnyashni vyechir?

do you have any family rooms? **for three nights**
у вас есть семейные номера? на трое суток
oo vas yes't' simyeïnyi namira? *na troye sootak*

would it be possible to add an extra bed?
можно будет поставить дополнительную кровать?
mozhna boodit pastavit' dapalnitil'nooyoo kravat'?

could I see the room first?
я могу вначале посмотреть номер?
ya magoo vnachali pasmatryet' nomir?

do you have anything bigger/quieter?
у вас есть номера побольше/потише?
oo vas yes't' namira pabol'she/patishe?

**is there air conditioning/a bath/a telephone/a television/a fridge
in the room?**
есть ли в номере кондиционер/ванна/телефон/телевизор/
холодильник?
yes't' li v nomirye kanditsyanyer/vana/tilifon/tilivizar/Haladil'nik?

that's fine, I'll take it
хорошо, этот номер мне подходит, я беру его
Harasho, etat nomir mne patHodit, ya biroo yivo

could you recommend any other hotels?
вы не могли бы посоветовать мне другую гостиницу?
vy ni magli by pasavyetavat' mne droogooyoo gastinitsoo?

is breakfast included? **is there a lift?**
завтрак включён в цену? где находится лифт?
zaftrak fklyoochon f tsenoo? *gdye naHoditsa lift?*

what time do you serve breakfast?
когда подаётся завтрак?
kagda padayotsa zaftrak?

is the hotel near the centre of town?
гостиница расположена рядом с центром?
gastinitsa raspalozhena ryadam s tsentram?

what time will the room be ready?
когда будет готов номер?
kagda boodit gatof nomir?

the key for room ..., please
дайте, пожалуйста, ключ от номера ...
daïti, pazhaloosta, klyooch at nomira ...

could I have an extra blanket?
можно попросить ещё одно одеяло?
mozhna paprasit' ischyo adno adiyala?

the air conditioning isn't working
кондиционер не работает
kanditsyanyer ni rabotait

could you please change the bed linen/towels?
пожалуйста, поменяйте постельное бельё/полотенце
pazhaloosta, paminyaïti pastyel'naya bil'yo/palatyentse

could you wake me up at ...
разбудите меня в ...
razbooditi minya v ...

can you please take my luggage to room number ...
пожалуйста, отнесите мой багаж в номер ...
pazhaloosta, atnisiti moï bagash v nomir ...

Understanding

номер с ванной/с балконом/ с видом на ...	room with bath/with balcony/with view of ...
стандартный номер	standard room
улучшенный номер	upgraded room
номер люкс	luxury room
апартаменты	apartments

извините, мест нет
izviniti, myest nyet
I'm sorry, but we're full

у нас свободны только одноместные номера
oo nas svabodny tol'ka adnamyesnyi namira
we only have single rooms available

сколько суток вы у нас пробудете?
na skol'ka sootak vy astanovitis'
how many nights will you be staying?

назовите ваше имя, пожалуйста
nazaviti vashe imya, pazhaloosta
what's your name, please?

вы можете заселиться начиная с 12 дня
vy mozhyti zasilitsa nachinaya s dvinatsati dnya
check-in is from midday

вам нужно освободить номер до 11 утра
vam noozhna asvabadit' nomir da adinatsati ootra
you have to check out before 11am

завтрак – с семи тридцати до девяти
zaftrak – s simi tritsati da diviti
breakfast is served in the restaurant between 7.30 and 9.00

ваш номер пока не готов
vash nomir paka ni gatof
your room isn't ready yet

вещи можно оставить здесь
vyeschi mozhna astavit' z'dyes
you can leave your bags here

SELF-CATERING

Expressing yourself

we're looking for somewhere to rent near a town
мы ищем что-нибудь недалеко от города
my ischem shto-niboot' nidaliko at gorada

where do we pick up/leave the keys?
где нужно оставлять/забирать ключи?
gdye noozhna astavlyat'/zabirat' klyoochi?

is electricity included in the price?
оплата электричества включена в цену?
aplata iliktrichistva fklyoochina v tsyenoo?

are bed linen and towels provided?
вы дадите нам бельё и полотенца?
vy daditi nam bil'yo i palatyentsa?

is the accommodation suitable for elderly people?
условия проживания подходят пожилым людям?
oosloviya prazhyvaniya patHodyat pazhylym lyoodyam?

where is the nearest supermarket?
где расположен ближайший магазин?
gdye raspalozhen blizhaïshy magazin?

how can we contact you?
как с вами можно связаться?
kak s vami mozhna svizatsa?

I can't find …
я не могу найти …
ya ni magoo naïti …

Understanding

если вам что-нибудь нужно, звоните мне по номеру …
yesli vam shto-niboot' noozhna, zvaniti mnye pa nomiroo
if you need anything, please give me a call in room …

квартира полностью меблирована
kvartira polnos't'yoo meblirovana
the flat is fully furnished

всё включено в цену
fsyo fklyoochino f tsenoo
everything is included in the price

CAMPING

Expressing yourself

is there a campsite near here?
недалеко отсюда есть кемпинг?
nidaliko atsyooda yes't' kempink?

I'd like to book a space for a two-person tent for three nights
мне нужно место для двухместной палатки на три ночи
mnye noozhna myesta dlya dvooHmyestnaï palatki na tri nochi

how much is it a night?
сколько стоит место в сутки?
skol'ka stoit myesta f sootki?

where is the shower block?
где находятся душевые?
gdye naHodyatsa dooshevyye?

can we pay, please? we were at space number ...
можно рассчитаться? мы жили на месте номер ...
mozhna raschitatsa? my zhyli na myesti nomir ...

Understanding

проживание стоит ... с человека в сутки
prazhyvaniye stoit... s chilavyeka f sootki
it's ... per person per night

если вам что-нибудь понадобиться, обращайтесь ко мне
yesli vam shto-niboot' panadabitsa, abraschyaïtis' ka mnye
if you need anything, just come and ask

EATING AND DRINKING   ¶|●

ⓘ

Many cafés, restaurants, bars and snack bars have sprung up since the fall of the Soviet Union. The independent restaurants which have replaced the old State-run establishments usually serve good quality and varied food. You can get a snack at a **столовая** (stalovaya) or a **буфет** (boofyet).

Most restaurants close around 11pm. Service is always included but you can still leave a tip (indeed, it is common practice in large restaurants). You should not drink the tap water; instead, drink mineral water, tea … or vodka!

To drink alcohol, go to a **бар** (bar), a bar that serves beer and light meals.

The basics

beer	пиво *piva*
bill	счёт *schyot*
black coffee	чёрный кофе *chyorny kofye*
bottle	бутылка *bootylka*
bread	хлеб *Hlyep*
breakfast	завтрак *zaftrak*
coffee	кофе *kofi*
Coke®	кола *kola*
dessert	десерт *disyert*
dinner	ужин *oozhyn*
fruit juice	(фруктовый) сок *(frooktovy) sok*
lemonade	лимонад *limanat*
lunch	обед *abyet*
main course	основное блюдо/горячее *asnavnoye blyooda/ garyachiye*
menu	меню *minyoo*
mineral water	минеральная вода *miniral'naya vada*
red wine	красное вино *krasnaye vino*
rosé wine	розовое вино *rozavaye vino*

44

salad	салат *salat*
sandwich	бутерброд *bootirbrot*
sparkling	(water) газированный *gazirovany*; (wine) игристый *igristy*
starter	закуска *zakooska*
still	(water) без газа *biz gaza*
tea	чай *chyaï*
tip	чаевые *chiivyye*
waiter	официант *afitsyyant*
waitress	официантка *afitsyyantka*
water	вода *vada*
white coffee	кофе с молоком *kofye s malakom*, со сливками *sa slifkami*
white wine	белое вино *byelaye vino*
wine	вино *vino*
wine list	карта вин *karta vin*
to eat	есть *yes't'*
to have breakfast	завтракать *zaftrakat'*
to have dinner	ужинать *oozhynat'*
to have lunch	обедать *abyedat'*
to order	заказывать *zakazyvat'*

Expressing yourself

shall we go and have something to eat?
давайте зайдём куда-нибудь перекусим?
davaïti zaïdyom kooda-niboot' pirikoosim?

do you want to go for a drink?
не хотите зайти чего-нибудь выпить?
ni Hatiti zaïti chivo-niboot' vypit'?

can you recommend a good restaurant?
вы можете посоветовать хороший ресторан?
vy mozhyti pasavyetyvat' Haroshy ristaran?

I'm not very hungry
я не очень голоден *(m)*/голодна *(f)*
ya ni ochin' goladin/galadna

cheers!
Ваше здоровье!
vashe zdarov'ye!

that was really delicious
Всё было очень вкусно
fsyo byla ochin' fkoosna

could you bring us an ashtray, please?
можете принести нам пепельницу, пожалуйста?
mozhyti prinisti nam pyepil'nitsoo, pazhaloosta?

where are the toilets, please?
вы не подскажете, где здесь туалет?
vy ni patskazhyti, gdye z'dyes' tooalyet?

Understanding

бизнес ланч	business lunch
кафе	café
доставка пиццы/суши	pizza/sushi delivery
пиццерия	pizzeria
ресторан	restaurant
на вынос	takeaway

извините, мы не обслуживаем после одиннадцати
izviniti, my ni apsloozhyvaim
I'm sorry, we stop serving at 11pm

RESERVING A TABLE

Expressing yourself

I'd like to reserve a table for tomorrow evening
я хочу заказать столик на завтра на вечер
ya Hachyoo zakazat' stolik na zaftra na vyechir

around 8 o'clock
приблизительно на восемь
priblizitil'na na vosim' vyechira

for two/four people
на двоих/на четверых вечера
na dvaiH/na chitviryH

I've reserved a table – the name's …
у нас заказан столик на имя …
oo nas zakazan stolik na imya …

Understanding

зарезервировано
reserved

на какое время?
na kakoye vryemya?
for what time?

 на сколько человек?
na skol'ka chilavyek?
for how many people?

на чьё имя?
na ch-yo imya?
what's the name?

 у вас заказан столик?
oo vas zakazan stolik?
do you have a reservation?

для курящих или для не курящих?
dlya kooryaschiH ili nikooryaschiH?
smoking or non-smoking?

вам подойдёт этот столик в углу?
vam padaidyot etat stolik v oogloo?
is this table in the corner OK for you?

к сожалению, на данный момент у нас нет свободных мест
k sazhylyeniyoo, na dany mamyent oo nas nyet svabodnyH myest
I'm afraid we're fully booked at the moment

ORDERING FOOD

Expressing yourself

do you have an English menu?
у вас есть меню на английском языке?
oo vas yes't' minyoo na angliskam yizykye?

what drink/main course could you recommend?
что вы нам можете посоветовать из напитков/горячего?
shto vy nam mozhyiti pasavyetavat' iz napitkaf/garyachiva?

I'm allergic to nuts/wheat/seafood/citrus fruit
у меня аллергия на орехи/пшеницу/морепродукты/цитрусовые
oo minya alirgiya na aryeHi/pshynitsoo/moripradookty/tsytroosavyi

yes, we're ready to order
да, мы уже выбрали
da, my oozhe vybrali

no, could you give us a few more minutes?
нет пока, нам нужно ещё несколько минут
nyet paka, nam noozhna ischyo nyeskal'ka minoot

I'd like …
я буду …
ya boodoo …

could I have …?
можно мне …?
mozhna mnye …?

what local specialities do you have?
какие у вас есть национальные блюда?
kakii oo vas yes't' natsyanal'nyi blyooda?

I'm not sure, what's "solyanka"?
я плохо представляю, что такое "солянка"?
ya ploHa pritstavlyayoo, shto takoye salyanka?

what does that dish come with?
какой гарнир подаётся к этому блюду?
kakoï garnir padayotsa k etamoo blyoodoo?

what's today's special?
какое у вас сегодня блюдо дня?
kakoye oo vas sivodnya blyooda dnya?

what desserts do you have?
какие у вас десерты?
kakii oo vas disyerty?

a bottle of red/white wine
бутылку белого/красного вина, пожалуйста
bootylkoo byelava/krasnava vina, pazhaloosta

some water/juice, please
стакан воды/сока, пожалуйста
stakan vady/soka, pazhaloosta

that's for me
это мне
eta mnye

this isn't what I ordered, I wanted …
я заказал *(m)*/заказала *(f)* не это, а …
ya zakazal/a ni eta, a …

could we have some more bread, please?
принесите нам, пожалуйста, ещё немного хлеба
prinisiti nam, pazhaloosta, ischyo nimnoga Hlyeba

could you bring us another jug of water, please?
принесите нам, пожалуйста, ещё графин воды
prinisiti nam, pazhaloosta, ischyo grafin vady

Understanding

блюдо от шеф повара	chef's recommendation
холодные закуски	cold snacks/starters
напитки	drinks
рыбные блюда	fish dishes
горячие закуски	hot snacks/starters
мясные блюда	meat dishes
блюда из птицы	poultry dishes
салаты	salads
супы	soups

вы уже выбрали?
vy oozhe vybrali?
are you ready to order?

что вы будете пить?
shto vy booditi pit'?
what would you like to drink?

я вернусь через несколько минут
ya virnoos' chiriz nyeskal'ka minoot
I'll come back in a few minutes

к сожалению, у нас закончился/закончилась …
k sazhylyeniyoo, oo nas zakonchilsya/zakonchilas'…
I'm sorry, we don't have any … left

хотите кофе или что-нибудь на десерт?
Hatiti kofi ili shto-niboot' na disyert?
would you like dessert or coffee?

BARS AND CAFÉS

Expressing yourself

I'd like …
я буду …
ya boodoo …

a glass of white/red wine
бокал красного/белого вина
bakal krasnava/byelava vina

a black/white coffee
один эспрессо/один кофе с молоком/каппучино
adin espresa/adin kofi s malakom/kapoochina

a coffee and a cake
чашку кофе и пирожное
chyashkoo kofi i pirozhnaye

the same again, please
то же самое, пожалуйста
to zhe samaya, pazhaloosta

a Coke®/a diet Coke®
колу/диетическую колу
koloo/diitichiskooyoo koloo

a cup of tea with lemon
один чай с лимоном
adin chyaï s limonam

a cup of hot chocolate
горячий шоколад, пожалуйста
garyachi shykalat, pazhaloosta

Understanding

безалкогольный   non-alcoholic

что вы будете заказывать?
shto vy booditi zakazyvat'?
what would you like?

здесь столики для некурящих
z'dyes' stoliki dlya nikooryaschiH
this is the non-smoking area

вы не могли бы заплатить сразу?
vy ni magli by zaplatit' srazoo?
could I ask you to pay now, please?

Some informal expressions

заморить червячка to have a bite to eat
объесться/натрескаться to overeat
пропустить стаканчик to have a few drinks
наклюкаться/перебрать to drink to excess
голова гудит с похмелья my head is throbbing from a hangover

THE BILL

Expressing yourself

the bill, please
счёт, пожалуйста/рассчитайте нас, пожалуйста
schyot, pazhaloosta/raschitaiti nas, pazhaloosta

how much do I owe you?
сколько я вам должен *(m)*/должна *(f)*?
skol'ka ya vam dolzhyn/dalzhna?

do you take credit cards?
вы принимаете кредитные карты?
vy prinimaiti kriditnyye karty?

I think there's a mistake in the bill
мне кажется, в счёте ошибка
mnye kazhytsa, f schyoti ashypka

is service included?
обслуживание включено в цену?
apsloozhyvanii fklyoochino v tsenoo?

Understanding

вам считать вместе?
vam schitat' vmyes'ti?
are you all paying together?

да, обслуживание включено в цену
da, apsloozhyvaniye fklyoochino f tsenoo
yes, service is included

FOOD AND DRINK ♟♟

(i)

Breakfast **завтрак** *(zaftrak)* is often substantial (sausages, eggs, cereal etc), while lunch **обед** *(abyet)* tends to be a light snack (sandwiches and tea). Lunch is generally eaten between 12 and 3pm and dinner **ужин** *(oozhyn)* between 7 and 10pm. Families get together in the evening for the main meal of the day. It usually consists of a hot or cold starter **закуска** *(zakooska)*, a main course **второе блюдо** *(ftaroye blyooda)* and a dessert **третье блюдо** *(tryetye blyooda)*. Cheese is sometimes served as a starter, but never before or in place of dessert. Tea is often served with dessert. Traditional Russian cuisine is based around potatoes, cabbage and grains, but now there is a wide variety of food to choose from.

Understanding

варёный *varyony*	boiled
во фритюре *va frityoori*	fried
горячий *garyachi*	hot
жареный *zhariny*	roasted, fried, grilled
печёный *pichyony*	baked
замороженный *zamarozhyny*	frozen
копчёный *kapchyony*	smoked
острый *ostry*	spicy
плавленый *plavliny*	processed
полуфабрикат *poloofabrikat*	prepared food, convenience foods
припущенный *pripooschyeny*	boiled
пюре *pyoore*	puree
с кровью *s krov'yoo*	rare *(meat)*
свежий *svyezhy*	fresh
сушёный *sooshony*	dried
тушёный *tooshony*	stewed
фаршированный *farshyrovany*	stuffed
холодный *Halodny*	cold

◆ **закуски** appetizers

салаты *salaty*	salads
оливье *aliv'ye*	salad with vegetables (potatoes, carrots, onion, green peas and pickles) and meat, dressed with mayonnaise
винегрет *vinigryet*	salad made from beetroot and the same vegetables as *aliv'ye*, but without meat
икра *ikra*	caviar, often served with pancakes
жульен *zhool'yen*	casserole of small mushrooms
грибы в сметане *griby v smitani*	mushrooms in sour cream
пирожок *pirazhok*	patty, pie
холодец *Haladyets*	jellied meat
греческий салат *gryechiski*	Greek salad
салат «Цезарь» *salat tsezar*	Caesar salad
селёдка под шубой *silyotka pat shoobaï*	dressed herring

◆ **первые блюда** first courses

супы *soopy*	soups
борщ *borsch'*	borscht (beetroot soup, often served with sour cream and sometimes with lemon)
щи *schi*	soup made from cabbage, carrots, potatoes, onion and meat
зелёные щи *zilyonyye schi*	soup with fresh sorrel, served with sour cream and hard-boiled eggs
бульон *bool'yon*	beef or chicken broth, served with toast or patties
уха *ooHa*	traditional fish soup with potatoes
солянка *salyanka*	traditional soup with tomatoes, pieces of meat, ham, small sausages, pickled cucumbers, olives and sometimes mushrooms
окрошка *akroshka*	cold soup with sour *kvas*, sausage, potatoes, fresh cucumbers, radish and spring onion, served with sour cream
суп-пюре *soop-pyoore*	creamy soup

◆ вторые блюда main courses

мясо *myasa*	meat
рыба *ryba*	fish
птица *ptitsa*	poultry
гарнир *garnir*	garnish
бефстроганов *bifstroganaf*	beef Stroganoff
пельмени *pil'myeni*	type of ravioli stuffed with meat
котлеты *katlyety*	rissoles
котлеты по-киевски *katlyety pa kiifski*	baked breast of chicken stuffed with butter sauce
плов *plof*	pilaf (rice dish made with mutton, carrots, onion and sometimes dried fruits and spices)
голубцы *galooptsy*	cabbage leaves stuffed with minced meat and onion
вареники *varyeniki*	ravioli filled with soft cheese, cherries, mushrooms or meat
шашлык *shashlyk*	barbecued mutton, pork or fish with grilled vegetables
фаршированный перец *farshyrovany pyerits*	pepper stuffed with minced meat in sauce
блины *bliny*	pancakes

◆ сладкие блюда desserts

мороженое *marozhynaye*	ice cream
мороженое ванильное *marozhynaye vanil'naye*	vanilla ice cream
мороженое фруктовое *marozhynaye frooktovaye*	fruit ice cream
мороженое шоколадное *marozhynaye shakaladnaye*	chocolate ice cream
торт *tort*	cake
пирожное *pirozhnaye*	small cake
пирожное «Картошка» *pirozhnaye kartoshka*	traditional Russian cake
наполеон *napalion*	large layered pastry and cream cake
эклер *shakaladny yklyer*	chocolate eclair

медовик *midavik*	type of tart made with biscuit and honey
ватрушка *vatrooshka*	sweet cake made with cottage cheese
пряники *pryaniki*	spice cake
желе *zhylye*	jelly
кисель *kisyel'*	type of blancmange

♦ **напитки** drinks

ⓘ

The most common brands of mineral water are **Святой источник** (*svitoï istochnik*) and **Новотерская** (*navatyerskaya*). You can also buy very salty fizzy water such as **Боржоми** (*barzhomi*), **Нарзан** (*narzan*), **Архыз** (*arHys*) and **Ессентуки** (*isyntooki*) in shops, at markets and in pharmacies.

Tea **чай** (*chyaï*) is very popular in Russia: it is drunk after every meal and throughout the day. Try the different varieties, including **Краснодарский** (*krasnadarski*), **Майский чай** (*maïski chyaï*), **Беседа** (*bisyeda*) and the Georgian tea **Грузинский** (*groozinski*).

The main Russian beers are **Старый мельник** (*stary myel'nik*), **Клинское** (*klinskaye*), **Балтика** (*baltika*), **Золотая бочка** (*zalataya bochka*), **Сибирская корона** (*sibirskaya karona*) and **Арсенальное** (*arsinal'naye*). Another very popular drink is **квас** (*kvas*), a slightly sweet and tangy soft drink made from water, black rye bread and malt.

If you want to buy vodka, it's best to do so in supermarkets rather than at markets. Some of the big names are **Московская** (*maskofskaya*), **Столичная** (*stalichnaya*), **Гжелка** (*gzhelka*), **Путинка** (*pootinka*) and **Юрий Долгорукий** (*yuri Dalgarooki*). Cognac and wine are also commonly drunk.

GLOSSARY OF FOOD AND DRINK

абрикос apricot	**апельсиновый сок** orange juice
авокадо avocado	**арбуз** watermelon
азу minced beef in sauce with pickles	**ассорти мясное** assorted meat
алкогольные напитки spirits	**ассорти овощное vegetable** assorted vegetables
ананас pineapple	
апельсин orange	**баклажан** aubergine

банан banana
баранина mutton, lamb
белок egg white
белый хлеб white bread
бифштекс steak
бифштекс с луком steak with onions
блинчики с вареньем pancakes with jam
бородинский хлеб rye bread with caraway seeds
буженина cold baked pork
булочка roll
бульон с клёцками broth with dumplings
бульон с фрикадельками broth with meatballs
бутерброд sandwich
варенье jam
ветчина ham
вишня cherry
виноград grapes
водка vodka
второе блюдо main course
гамбургер hamburger
говядина beef
горох peas
горчица mustard
грейпфрут grapefruit
грецкий орех walnut
грибы mushrooms
маринованные грибы pickled mushrooms
грудинка bacon
груша pear
гуляш beef goulash
гусь жареный roast goose
гусь с яблоками roast goose stuffed with apples
дыня melon
жареное филе рыбы baked fillet of fish

жареные кабачки roast marrow
жареный картофель fried potato
жаркое с овощами roast meat with vegetables
желток egg yolk
закуска snack
заливная рыба jellied fish
замороженные продукты frozen foods
запеканка картофельная baked potato pudding
запеканка творожная home-made baked cheesecake, often with raisins
зелёная фасоль green haricot beans
зелёный горошек peas
изюм raisins
икра баклажанная aubergine puree
икра кабачковая marrow puree
икра красная red caviar
икра чёрная black caviar
индейка turkey
йогурт yogurt
кальмары squid
камбала flat fish
капуста cabbage
карп жареный roast carp
картофель potatoes
картофельное пюре mashed potatoes
каша гречневая boiled buckwheat
каша геркулесовая boiled porridge
каша манная semolina
каша пшённая millet porridge
квашеная капуста sauerkraut
кекс fruit cake
кета Siberian salmon
кетчуп ketchup
кефир kefir (yoghurt drink)
клубника strawberries
кофе coffee

кофе в зёрнах coffee beans
кофе с молоком white coffee
колбаса sausage
компот drink made from stewed fruit
краб crab
креветка shrimp
кролик rabbit
кукуруза maize, sweetcorn
курица chicken
лаваш Georgian white bread
лапша молочная noodles in hot milk
лапша грибная noodles with mushrooms
лапша куриная chicken noodle soup
ликёр liqueur
лимон lemon
лимонад lemonade
лосось salmon
лук onion
майонез mayonnaise
макароны macaroni
малина raspberries
мандарин mandarin
маргарин margarine
масло butter
мёд honey
миндаль almond
молоко milk
морепродукты seafood
морковь carrots
мороженое ice cream
мука flour
мясо meat
овощи vegetables
овощной суп vegetable soup
овсяные хлопья cornflakes
огурец cucumber
оладьи fritters
оливки olives
омар lobster
омлет scrambled egg, omelette

орех nut
осетрина sturgeon
отбивная chop; **свиная отбивная** pork chop
отварная курица boiled chicken
отварное мясо boiled meat
паштет pâté
перец pepper
персик peach
песочное пирожное shortbread
печёнка liver
печень трески в масле cod liver oil
печенье biscuits
пиво beer; **пиво разливное** draft beer
пирог pie; **яблочный пирог** apple pie
пирожки с капустой cabbage patties
пирожки с мясом meat patties
пирожное cake
пицца pizza
помидор tomato
пончики doughnuts
приправа seasoning
рагу stew
рак crayfish
рассольник soup with pickles and pearl barley
растворимый кофе instant coffee
растительное масло oil
рис rice
рыба fish
салат salad
салат из огурцов cucumber salad
салат из помидоров tomato salad
сарделька type of sausage
сардина sardine
сахар sugar
сахарный песок granulated sugar

свекольник cold soup with beetroot, potatoes and fresh cucumber
свинина pork
сгущённое молоко, сгущёнка sweetened condensed milk
селёдка herring
сёмга salmon trout
сидр cider
скумбрия mackerel
сладкий sweet
слива plum
сливки cream
сметана sour cream
сок juice
солёные огурцы pickled cucumbers
солёный salted
сосиска sausage
соус sauce
судак pike, perch
суп soup
суп гороховый с беконом pea soup with bacon
суп грибной mushroom soup
суп картофельный potato soup
сушки ring-shaped rusk biscuits
сыр cheese
творог cottage cheese
телятина veal
тесто pastry
тесто песочное shortcrust pastry
тесто слоёное puff pastry
тефтели meatballs in tomato sauce
треска жареная roast cod
тушёное мясо в горшочке meat stewed in a clay pot
уксус vinegar
устрица oyster
утка duck
фаршированные помидоры stuffed tomato (with garlic, parsley and feta cheese)

фасоль haricot beans
финик date
филе окуня perch fillet
форель trout
фруктовый сок fruit juice
харчо spicy lamb soup
хлопья breakfast cereals
цветная капуста cauliflower
цыплёнок табака roast spatchcock chicken with garlic, parsley and dill sauce
чай tea
чебурек fried dumpling stuffed with meat or cheese or potatoes and mushrooms
чёрная смородина blackcurrants
чёрный хлеб black bread
чеснок garlic
чеснок маринованный pickled garlic
чипсы chips, crisps
шаурма chopped meat (pork or chicken), fresh cabbage, carrots, tomatoes etc in cream and tomato sauce, rolled in thin dough
шашлык barbecued kebab on skewer
шоколад chocolate
молочный горячий milk chocolate
молочный чёрный hot chocolate
молочный шоколад dark chocolate
шпинат spinach
шпроты sprats
щи из кислой капусты sauerkraut soup
яблоко apple
язык отварной ox tongue
яичница fried egg
яйцо egg
яйцо вкрутую hard-boiled egg
яйцо всмятку soft-boiled egg
яйцо под майонезом egg mayonnaise

GOING OUT

To find out what's on in Moscow, see the **Moscow Times** (free daily paper) or **Moscow Magazine** (bi-monthly magazine), both of which are in English. The equivalent in Saint Petersburg is **Neva News**.

Russians have always loved theatre, concerts and ballet. Although ticket prices are now too high for the average Russian, many people still enjoy such entertainment. Moscow and Saint Petersburg are meccas for lovers of art, music and dance. In Moscow, you can choose between the Bolshoi (*bal'shoï*), the Stanislavski (*stanislavski*) Theatre or the Grand Kremlin Palace. Saint Petersburg boasts the Mariinsky (*mariïnski*) Theatre, the Maly (*maly*) Theatre and the Grand Philharmonic for concerts. Be warned that prices are often doubled or even tripled for foreigners.

There are plenty of cinemas, but the lack of resources in Russian studios means that few national productions are screened.

Some hotels have discos, and many restaurants put on dinner dances. Pubs and jazz clubs tend to attract a young, fairly wealthy crowd.

Russians love having guests, and if you are lucky enough to be invited to someone's house you will experience true Russian hospitality. Never arrive empty-handed – if you don't have any small gifts from back home, bring some food, drink or flowers. Always give an odd number of flowers unless it's a sad occasion.

The basics

ballet	балет *balyet*
band	оркестр *arkyestr*
bar	бар *bar*
cinema	кино *kino*
circus	цирк *tsyrk*
classical music	классическая музыка *klassichiskaya moozyka*
club	клуб *kloop*
concert	концерт *kantsert*

concert hall	концертный зал *kantsertny zal*
conductor	дирижёр *dirizhor*
conservatoire	консерватория *kansirvatoriya*
dubbed film	дублированный фильм *doobliravany fil'm*
festival	фестиваль *fistival'*
film	фильм *fil'm*
folk music	народная музыка *narodnaya moozyka*
group	группа *groopa*
jazz	джаз *dzhas*
musical	мюзикл *myoozikl*
opera	опера *opira*
party	вечеринка *vichirinka*
play	играть *igrat'*
pop music	поп-музыка *pop-moozyka*
rock music	рок-музыка *rok-moozyka*
show	шоу *sho-oo*
subtitled film	фильм с субтитрами *fil'm s sooptitrami*
theatre	театр *tiatr*
ticket	билет *bilyet*

SUGGESTIONS AND INVITATIONS

Expressing yourself

where can we go?
куда пойдём?
kooda païdyom?

what do you want to do?
чем бы вы хотели заняться?
chyem by vy Hatyeli zanyatsa?

shall we go for a drink?
может быть, зайдём, выпьем чего-нибудь?
mozhyt byt' zaïdyom vyp'im chivo-niboot'?

do you have plans?
у вас есть планы на вечер?
oo vas yes't' plany na vyechir?

what are you doing tonight?
что вы делаете сегодня вечером?
shto vy dyelaiti sivodnya vyechiram?

would you like to …?
вы не хотели бы …?
vy ni Hatyeli by …?

we were thinking of going to …
мы собираемся пойти в …
my sabiraimsya païti v …

I'm not sure I can make it
вряд ли я смогу
vryat li ya smagoo

I'd love to
с удовольствием
s oodavol'stviyem

ARRANGING TO MEET

Expressing yourself

how shall we arrange it?
как мы договоримся?
kak my dagavarimsya?

what time shall we meet?
когда мы встретимся?
kagda my fstryetimsya?

where shall we meet?
где мы встретимся?
gdye my fstryetimsya?

would it be possible to meet a bit later?
давай встретимся попозже?
davaï fstryetimsya papozhe?

I have to meet ... at nine
мы договорились встретиться с ... в 9
my dagavarilis' fstryetitsa s ... v dyevit'

I don't know where it is but I'll find it on the map
я не знаю, где это, но могу посмотреть по карте
ya ni znayoo, gdye eta, no magoo pasmatryet' pa karti

see you tomorrow night!
тогда встретимся завтра вечером!
tagda fstryetimsya zaftra vyechiram!

I'll call/text you if there's a change of plan
я позвоню/напишу СМС, если что-нибудь изменится
ya pazvanyoo/napishoo SMS, yesli shto-niboot' izmyenitsa

sorry I'm late
извините за опоздание
izviniti za apazdanyei

Understanding

вам это удобно?
vam eta oodobna?
is that OK with you?

я вас там встречу
ya vas tam fstryechoo
I'll meet you there

я заеду за вами около восьми
ya zayedoo za vami okala vas'mi
I'll come and pick you up about 8

можем встретиться снаружи/у входа
mozhym fstryetitsa snaroozhy/oo fHoda
we can meet outside/near the entrance

запишите мой номер и вы сможете мне позвонить завтра
zapishyti moï nomir i vy smozhyti mnye pazvanit' zaftra
I'll give you my number and you can call me tomorrow

Some informal expressions

пропустить по стаканчику to go for a drink
перекусить/перехватить что-нибудь to have a bite to eat

FILMS, SHOWS AND CONCERTS

Expressing yourself

what time does the film/the show start?
когда начало сеанса/представления?
kagda nachala syansa/pritstavlyeniya?

does the show have an interval?
спектакль идёт с антрактом?
spiktakl' idyot s antraktam?

is there a guide to what's on?
где можно найти афишу/репертуар театра?
gdye mozhna naïti afishoo/ripirtooar tyatra?

two tickets, please
два билета, пожалуйста
dva bilyeta, pazhaloosta

are there tickets available for today?
есть ли билеты на сегодня?
yest' li bilyety na sivodnya?

I'd like three cheap/good tickets for …
мне нужно три недорогих/хороших билета на …
mnye noozhna tri nidaragiH/HaroshyH bilyeta na …

I'll find out whether there are tickets available
я узнаю, можно ли достать билеты
ya ooznayoo, mozhna li dastat' bilyety

do we need to book in advance?
билеты нужно заказывать заранее?
bilyety noozhna zakazyvat' zaraniye

how long is the film/play on for?
как давно идёт этот фильм/спектакль?
kak davno idyot etat fil'm/spiktakl'?

I'd like to go to a bar with some live music
я бы хотел *(m)*/хотела *(f)* пойти в кафе/бар, где играет живая
музыка
ya by Hatyel/Hatyela paiti v kafe/bar, gdye igrait zhyvaya moozyka

are there any free concerts?
проводятся ли бесплатные концерты?
pravodyatsa li bisplatnyye kantserty?

Understanding

амфитеатр	circle
балкон	balcony
буфет	bar
во всех кинотеатрах с …	on general release from …
дневной спектакль	matinée
кассы	box office
ложа	box
малая/большая сцена	large/small stage

на сегодня все спектакли   all today's performances are cancelled
  отменяются
премьера   first night
расписание сеансов   programme of performances

к сожалению, все билеты проданы
k sazhylyeniyu, fsye bilyety prodany
unfortunately, that showing's sold out

билеты можно не бронировать заранее
bilyety mozhna ni braniryvat' zaraniye
there's no need to book in advance

спектакль идет полтора часа включая антракт
spiktakl' idyot paltara chisa fklyuchyaya antrakt
the play lasts an hour and a half, including the interval

вам какие места?   **вам показать ваши места?**
vam kakii mista?   *vam pakazat' vashy mista?*
which seats would you like?   shall I show you where your seats are?

приятного просмотра!   **не хотите купить программу?**
priyatnava prasmotra!   *ni Hatiti koopit' pragramoo?*
enjoy the show!   would you like to buy a programme?

на время спектакля убедительная просьба выключить
  сигналы Ваших мобильных телефонов
na vryemya spiktaklya oobiditil'naya proz'ba vyklyoochit' signaly vashyH
  mabil'nyH tilifonaf
please turn off your mobile phone during the performance

PARTIES AND CLUBS

Expressing yourself

I'm having a little leaving party tonight
сегодня вечером я устраиваю прощальную вечеринку
sivodnya vyechiram ya oostraivayoo praschyal'nooyoo vichirinkoo

should I bring something to drink?
мне принести что-нибудь выпить?
mnye prinisti shto-niboot' vypit'?

we could go to a club afterwards
потом мы можем пойти в клуб
patom my mozhym paiti f kloop

do you have to pay to get in?
вход платный?
fHot platny?

I have to meet someone inside
меня ждут внутри
minya zhdoot vnootri

will you let me back in when I come back?
вы меня пропустите, когда я вернусь?
vy minya prapoostiti, kagda ya virnoos'?

no thanks, I don't smoke
спасибо, но я не курю
spasiba, no ya ni kooryoo

can I buy you a drink?
хочешь чего-нибудь выпить?
Hochish' chivo-niboot' vypit'?

thanks, but I'm not on my own
спасибо, но я здесь не один *(m)*/одна *(f)*
spasiba, no ya z'dyes' ni adin/adna

Understanding

гардероб	cloakroom
круглосуточно	round the clock
напиток бесплатно	free drink

у Анны сегодня будет вечеринка
oo any sivodnya boodit vichirinka
there's a party today at Anna's place

потанцуем?
patantsooim?
do you want to dance?

у вас есть зажигалка?
oo vas yes't' zazhygalka?
have you got a light?

у вас не будет сигареты?
oo vas ni boodit sigaryety?
have you got any cigarettes?

мы увидимся снова?
my oovidimsya snova?
can we see each other again?

могу я проводить вас домой?
magoo ya pravadit' vas damoï?
can I see you home?

TOURISM AND SIGHTSEEING

TOURISM, SIGHTSEEING

The basics

ancient	древний *dryevni*
antique	античный *antichny*
castle	замок *zamak*
cathedral	собор *sabor*, храм *Hram*
century	век *vyek*
chapel	часовня *chisovnya*
church	церковь *tserkaf'*
exhibition	выставка *vystafka*
folk art	народное творчество *narodnaye tvorchistva*
fountain	фонтан *fantan*
gallery	галерея *galiryeya*
modern art	современное искусство *savrimyenaya iskoostva*
monastery	монастырь *manastyr'*
monument	памятник *pamitnik*
museum	музей *moozyeï*
painting	живопись *zhyvapis'*
park	парк *park*
ruins	развалины *razvaliny*
sculpture	скульптура *skool'ptoora*
square	площадь *ploschit'*
statue	статуя *statooya*
streetmap	карта города *karta gorada*

tour guide	путеводитель *pootivaditil'*
tourist	турист *toorist*
tourist information centre	экскурсионное бюро *ikskoorsionaya byooro*
town centre	центр города *tsentr gorada*

Expressing yourself

I'd like some information on …
я бы хотел получить какие-нибудь сведения о …
ya by Hatyel paloochit' kakii-niboot' svediniya a …

can you tell me where the tourist information centre is?
вы не подскажите, где здесь экскурсионное бюро?
vy ni patskazhyti, gdye z'dyes' ikskoorsiyonaye byooro?

do you have a streetmap of the town?
у вас есть карта/план города?
oo vas yes't' karta/plan gorada?

I was told there's a museum/monument around here
мне сказали, здесь неподалёку есть музей/памятник
mnye skazali, z'dyes' nipadalyokoo yes't' moozyei/pamitnik

can you show me where it is on the map?
вы можете показать мне это на карте?
vy mozhyti pakazat' mnye eta na karti?

how do you get there?
как можно туда пройти?
kak mozhna tooda praïti?

is it free to go in?
вход свободный?
fHot svabodny?

when was it built?
когда он построен *(m)* /она построена *(f)* /оно построено *(n)* ?
kagda on pastroin/ana pastroina/ano pastroina?

where is the ticket office?
где находится касса?
gdye naHoditsa kasa?

do you have an English-speaking guide?
есть ли гид, говорящий по-английски?
yes't' li git, gavaryaschi pa-angliski?

Understanding

вход свободный	admission free
закрыто	closed
древнерусский	old Russian
икона	icon
средневековый	medieval
открыто	open
закрыто на реставрацию	closed for restoration work
экскурсия	guided tour
вы находитесь здесь	you are here *(on a map)*

вам надо будет узнать на месте
vam nada boodit ooznat' na myes'ti
you'll have to ask when you get there

следующая экскурсия на английском состоится в два часа
slyedooschiya ikskoorsiya na angliiskam sastaitsa v dva chisa
the next guided tour in English starts at 2 o'clock

MUSEUMS, EXHIBITIONS AND MONUMENTS

Expressing yourself

what exhibitions are there in town at the moment?
какие выставки идут сейчас в городе?
kakii vystafki idoot sichyas v goradi?

I've heard there's a very good ... exhibition on at the moment
я слышал, сейчас проходит очень хорошая выставка,
  посвящённая …
ya slyshal, sichyas praHodit ochin' Haroshaya vystafka, pasvyaschonaya …

how much is it to get in?
сколько стоит входной билет?
skol'ka stoit fHadnoï bilyet?

how long does the excursion last?
сколько длится экскурсия?
skol'ka dlitsa ikskoorsiya?

is this ticket valid for the exhibition as well?
по этому билету можно пройти на выставку?
pa etamoo bilyetoo mozhna praïti na vystafkoo?

are there any discounts for young people?
есть ли скидки для школьников и студентов?
yes't li skitki dlya shkol'nikaf i stoodyentaf?

is it open on Sundays?
в воскресение открыто?
v vaskrisyeniye atkryta?

I have a student card
у меня есть студенческий билет
oo minya yes't stoodyenchiski bilyet

two concessions and one full price, please
два льготных и один полный билет, пожалуйста
dva l'gotnyH i adin polny bilyet, pazhaloosta

Understanding

аудиогид	audioguide
временная экспозиция	temporary exhibition
касса	ticket office
начало осмотра	start of the tour
не фотографировать	no photography
постоянная экспозиция	permanent exhibition
продолжение осмотра	continuation of the tour
руками не трогать	please do not touch
соблюдайте тишину	silence, please
фотографировать со вспышкой запрещено	no flash photography

входной билет в музей стоит …
fHadnoï bilyet v moozyeï stoit…
admission to the museum costs …

с этим билетом вы можете пройти на выставку
s etim bilyetam vy mozhyti praïti na vystafkoo
this ticket also allows you access to the exhibition

у вас есть студенческий билет?
oo vas yes't stoodyenchiski bilyet?
do you have your student card?

GIVING YOUR IMPRESSIONS

Expressing yourself

it's beautiful
красиво
krasiva

it's fantastic
потрясающе
patrisayoosche

I really enjoyed it
мне правда понравилось
mnye pravda panravilas'

I didn't like it that much
мне не очень понравилось
mnye ni ochin' panravilas'

it was a bit boring
было немного скучно
byla nimnoga skooshna

it's expensive for what it is
это не стоит таких денег
eta ni stoit takiH dyenik

I'm not really a fan of modern art
я не любитель современного искусства
ya ni lyoobitil' savrimyenava iskoostva

it was really crowded
было столько народу!
byla stol'ka narodoo!

it's very touristy
рассчитано больше на туристов
raschitana bol'shy na tooristaf

we didn't go in the end, the queue was too long
мы не дождались, было огромная очередь
my ni dazhdalis', byla agromnaya ochirit'

we didn't have time to see everything
мы не успели всё осмотреть
my ni oospyeli fsyo asmatryet'

Understanding

знаменитый	famous
живописный	picturesque
типичный	typical
традиционный	traditional

вам обязательно нужно посетить/посмотреть …
vam abizatil'na nada pasitit'/ pasmatryet'
you really must go and visit/see …

я бы посоветовал вам сходить в …
ya by pasavyetyval vam sHadit' v…
I recommend going to …

оттуда открывается чудесный вид на город
atooda atkryvaitsa chyoodyesny vit na gorat
there's a wonderful view over the whole city

это стало слишком туристическим местом
eta stala slishkam tooristichiskim myestam
it's become a bit too touristy

SPORTS AND GAMES

(i)

Russians particularly enjoy sports on ice: skating and ice hockey are very popular, as is cross-country skiing. Just as in Europe, football is also a major sport: Moscow has three excellent teams, **Lokomotif**, **Tseska** and **Spartak**, while the Saint Petersburg team is called **Zenit**.

Some people in Russia enjoy the alleged health benefits of diving through holes made in the ice into freezing water. This activity is particularly popular in Siberia, and the brave swimmers are known as *marzhy* (walruses). If you don't feel quite up to that, you can still enjoy a Russian bath *(banya)*: after a steam bath, people like to freshen up with a roll in the snow.

Board games, cards, dominoes, draughts and especially chess are still popular with young and old alike.

The basics

badminton	бадминтон *badminton*
ball	мяч *myach*
basketball	баскетбол *baskidbol*
board game	настольная игра *nastol'naya igra*
cards	карты *karty*
chess	шахматы *shaHmaty*
cross-country skiing	лыжи *lyzhy*
cycling	велосипедный спорт *vilasipyedny sport*
downhill skiing	горные лыжи *gornyye lyzhy*
football	футбол *foodbol*
gym	тренажёрный зал *trinazhorny zal*
hiking path	туристический маршрут *tooristichiski marshroot*
ice rink	каток *katok*
massage	массаж *masash*
match	матч *mach*
mountain biking	горный велосипед *gorny vyilasipyet*

pool *(game)*	бильярд *bil'yart*
racket	ракетка *rakyetka*
rugby	регби *regbi*
skates	коньки *kan'ki*
snowboarding	сноуборд *sno-oobort*
sport	спорт *sport*
sports hall	спортзал *sportzal*
swimming	плавание *plavaniye*
swimming pool	бассейн *basyeïn*
table football	настольный футбол *nastol'ny footbol*
table tennis	пинг-понг *pin-ponk*
team	команда *kamanda*
tennis	теннис *tenis*
tennis court	теннисный корт *tyenisny kort*
trip	поездка *payestka*
volleyball	волейбол *valibol*
to go hiking	ходить в походы *Hadit' v paHody*
to have a game of …	сыграть … *sygrat' …*
to play	играть *igrat'*

Expressing yourself

I'd like to hire … for an hour
я бы хотел *(m)*/хотела *(f)* взять напрокат … на час
ya by Hatyel/Hatyela vzyat' naprakat … na chyas

can I book a session with an instructor?
можно записаться на занятия с инструктором?
mozhna zapisatsa na zanyatiya s instrooktaram?

where is there a timetable of activities?
где можно узнать расписание занятий?
gdye mozhna ooznat' raspisanii zanyatiï

how much does it cost for a session?
сколько стоит одно занятие?
skol'ka stoit adno zanyatiye na myeits?

how much is it per person per hour?
какова цена за час с человека?
kakava tsyna za chyas s chilavyeka?

I'm not very fit
я не в очень хорошей форме
ya ni v ochin' Haroshyeï formi

I've never done it before
я никогда раньше этим не занимался *(m)*/занималась *(f)*
ya nikagda ran'she etim ni zanimalsya/zanimalas'

I've done it once or twice, a long time ago
я пробовал *(m)*/пробовала *(f)* пару раз когда-то давно
ya probaval/probavala paroo ras kagda-ta davno

I'm exhausted!
я очень устал *(m)*/устала *(f)*!
ya ochin' oostal/oostala!

I'd like to go and watch a football match
я хочу посмотреть футбольный матч
ya Hachyoo pasmatryet' footbol'ny match

Understanding

прокат ...   ... for hire

какими видами спорта вы занимаетесь?
kakimi vidami sporta vy zanimaitis'?
what kind of sport do you play?

расписание можно взять у администратора
raspisaniye mozhna vzyat' oo administratara
you can get the timetable from the administrator

у вас неплохо получается для первого раза
oo vas niploHa paloochyaitsa dlya pyervava raza
that's not bad for a first attempt

вы раньше этим занимались или будете начинать с нуля?
vy ran'she etim zanimalis' ili booditi nachinat' s noolya?
do you have any experience, or are you a complete beginner?

надо внести залог в размере ...
nada vnis'ti zalok v razmyeri
you need to pay a deposit of ...

страховка обязательна и стоит …
straHofka abizatil'na i stoit …
insurance is compulsory and costs …

HIKING

Expressing yourself

are there any hiking paths around here?
какие есть в окрестности туристические маршруты?
kakii yes't' v akryestnas'ti tooristichiskii marshrooty?

can you recommend any good walks in the area?
где здесь можно погулять?
gdye z'd'es' mozhna pagoolyat'?

do you have a map or a route plan?
у вас есть карта или схема маршрута?
oo vas yes't' karta ili sHyema marshroota?

can I hire hiking boots?
можно взять напрокат ботинки?
mozhna vzyat' naprakat batinki?

how long does the hike take?
на сколько часов рассчитан этот маршрут?
na skol'ka chisof raschitan etat marshroot?

is it very steep?
там подъём очень крутой?
tam pad-yom ochin' krootoi?

where's the start of the path?
где начало маршрута?
gdye nachala marshroota?

is the path signposted?
на тропе есть указатели?
na tropye yes't' ookazatili

is it a circular path?
это кольцевой маршрут?
eta kal'tsyvoї marshroot?

shall we stop for a break?
может быть, сделаем привал?
mozhyt byt', zdyelaim prival?

Understanding

средняя продолжительность average duration *(of walk)*

это примерно на три часа включая привалы
eta primyerna na tri chisa fklyuchaya privaly
it's about three hours' walk including stops

наденьте спортивную обувь и захватите с собой дождевик
nadyen'ti spartivnooyu oboof' i zaHvatiti s saboï dazhdivik
wear walking shoes and bring a waterproof jacket with you

SKIING, SKATING AND SNOWBOARDING

Expressing yourself

I'd like to hire skis, poles and boots/a snowboard/skates
Я хочу взять напрокат лыжи, палки и ботинки/сноуборд/коньки
ya Hachyoo vzyat' naprakat lyzhy, palki i batinki/sno-oobort/kan'ki

I need ... in a size ...	**they're too big/small**
мне нужен ... размер ...	они мне малы/велики
mnye noozhyn ... razmyer ...	*ani mnye maly/viliki*

I need a day pass/a pass for ... hours
мне нужен абонемент на день/на ... часов
mnye noozhyn abanimyent na dyen'/na ... chisof

where can I get changed/leave my things?
где можно переодеться/оставить вещи?
gdye mozhna pyiriadyetsa/astavit' vyeschi?

Understanding

бугельный подъёмник	T-bar ski lift
карточка/пропуск	lift pass
кресельный подъёмник	chair lift
фуникулёр	cable railway

OTHER SPORTS

Expressing yourself

where can we hire bikes?
где можно взять напрокат велосипеды?
gdye mozhna vzyat' naprakat vilasipyedy?

are there any cycle paths?
здесь есть велосипедные дорожки?
z'd'es' yes't' vilasipyednyi daroshki?

where can we have a game of football/volleyball/basketball/badminton?
где мы можем поиграть в футбол/волейбол/баскетбол/бадминтон?
gdye my mozhym paigrat' v foodbol/valibol/baskidbol/badminton?

which team do you support?   **I support …**
за какую команду вы болеете?   я болею за …
za kakooyoo kamandoo vy balyeiti?   *ya balyeyoo za …*

is there an open-air swimming pool?
здесь есть открытый бассейн?
z'dyes' yes't' atkryty basyein?

do you have any rackets?   **I run in the mornings**
у вас есть ракетки?   я бегаю по утрам
oo vas yes't' rakyetki?   *ya byegayoo pa ootram*

where can I have a shower?   **we want a court for two hours**
где можно принять душ?   мы хотим снять корт на два часа
gdye mozhna prinyat' doosh?   *my Hatim snyat' kort na dva chisa*

Understanding

резиновую шапочку и очки можете взять напрокат
rizinavayoo shapachkoo i achki mozhyti vzyat' naprakat
you can hire a swimming hat and goggles

вот ключ от вашего шкафчика
vot klyooch at vashyva shkafchika
here's the key to your locker

раздевалка на втором этаже
raz'divalka na ftarom ytazhe
changing rooms are on the first floor

теннисный корт занят до двух часов дня
tenisny kort zanyat da dvooH chisof dnya
the tennis court is occupied until two o'clock

вы умеете плавать?
vy oomeiti plavat'?
can you swim?

вы умеете играть в баскетбол?
vy oomeiti igrat' v baskidbol?
do you play basketball?

INDOOR GAMES

Expressing yourself

shall we have a game of cards/dominoes/bingo/chess/draughts?
сыграем в карты/домино/лото/шахматы/шашки?
sygraim v karty/damino/lato/shaHmaty/shashki?

do you know the rules?
вы знаете правила?
vy znaiti pravila?

it's your turn
твой/ваш ход
tvoï/vash Hot

Understanding

может быть, партию в бильярд?
mozhyd byt', partiyoo v bil'yart?
shall we have a game of pool?

вы умеете играть в шахматы?
vy oomyeiti igrat' f shaHmaty?
do you know how to play chess?

у вас есть карты?
oo vas yes't' karty?
do you have a pack of cards?

ничья
nich-ya
it's a draw

 **SHOPPING**

ℹ️

Shops are generally open from 8am to 8pm; some close for lunch from 1 to 2 or 2 to 3pm. Supermarkets are quite rare in Russia, except in big cities. There are several supermarket chains in Moscow: **Перекрёсток** (pirikryostak), **Копейка** (kapyeika), **Пятёрочка**, (pityorachka), **Рамстор** (ramstor) and **Билла** (bila). The supermarkets in Saint Petersburg are **Лента** (lyenta), **Карусель** (karoosyel'), **Пятерочка** (pityorochka) and **ОК** (okyei). You will find small shops and kiosks open 24 hours a day, selling drinks, biscuits and chocolate. Cigarettes are sold at tobacco kiosks **табачный киоск** (tabachny kiosk). There are plenty of daily markets selling clothes and food (fruit, vegetables etc). These are often located beside metro stations, and are cheaper than shops. A few famous department stores are **ГУМ** (goom), **Охотный ряд** (aHotny ryat), **Атриум** (atrioom) and **ЦУМ** (tsoom) in Moscow, and **Гостиный Двор** (gastiny dvor) and **Пассаж** (pasash) in Saint Petersburg.

When buying women's clothes, note that a UK size 12 (European 40) corresponds to a size 46 in Russia. For shoes, the European system of sizing is used, eg a UK size 6 will correspond to size 39.

Some informal expressions

цены кусаются prices are really high
цены упали prices slashed
это стоит безумно дорого it costs an arm and a leg
купить задаром/ почти за бесценок it's a real bargain
у меня нет ни копейки I'm skint

The basics

bakery	булочная *boolachnaya*
cash desk	касса *kasa*
cheap	дешёвый *dishyovy*
checkout	касса *kasa*
clothes	одежда *adyezhda*
department store	универмаг *oonivirmak*

discount card	дисконтная карта *diskontnaya karta*
expensive	дорогой *daragoï*
gram	грамм *gram*
greengrocer's	овощи и фрукты *ovaschi i frookty*
hypermarket	гипермаркет *gipirmarket*
kilo	килограмм *kilagram*
present	подарок *padarak*
price	цена *tsyna*
receipt	чек *chyek*
refund	возврат товара *vazvrat tavara*
sales	скидки *skitki*
sales assistant	продавец *pradavyets*
shoes	обувь *oboof'*
shop	магазин *magazin*
shopping centre	торговый центр *targovy tsentr*
souvenir	сувенир *soovinir*
supermarket	супермаркет *soopirmarkit*
to buy	покупать *pakoopat'*
to cost	стоить *stoit'*
to pay	платить *platit'*
to sell	продавать *pradavat'*

Expressing yourself

is there a supermarket near here?
тут поблизости есть супермаркет?
toot pablizas'ti yes't' soopirmarkit?

where can I buy cigarettes?
где я могу купить сигареты?
gdye ya magoo koopit' sigaryety?

I'd like …
я бы хотел *(m)*/хотела *(f)* …
ya by Hatyel/Hatyela …

I'm looking for/I need …
я ищу/мне нужно …
ya ischyoo/mnye noozhna …

do you sell …?
у вас есть …?
oo vas yes't' …?

how much is this?
сколько это стоит?
skol'ka eta stoit?

I'll take it
я это беру
ya eta biroo

I haven't got much money
у меня с собой не так много денег
oo minya s saboï ni tak mnoga dyenik

that's everything, thanks
это всё, спасибо
eta fsyo, spasiba

can I have a (plastic) bag?
можно попросить пакет?
mozhna paprasit' pakyet?

I think you've made a mistake with my change
мне кажется, вы неправильно дали сдачу
mnye kazhytsa, vy nipravil'na dali sdachyoo

Understanding

часы работы — opening hours
открыто с ... до ... — open from ... to ...
выходной: воскресение — closed on Sundays
обеденный перерыв с **13** до **14** — closed for lunch from 13.00 to 14.00
специальное предложение — special offer
скидки/распродажа — sale

это продаётся в другом отделе
eta pradayotsa v droogom adyeli
that's sold in another department

что-нибудь ещё?
shto-niboot' ischyo?
will there be anything else?

вам нужен пакет?
vam noozhyn pakyet?
would you like a bag?

PAYING

Expressing yourself

where do I pay?
где можно заплатить?
gdye mozhna zaplatit'?

how much do I owe you?
сколько я вам должен/должна?
skol'ka ya vam dolzhyn/dalzhna?

could you write it down for me, please?
напишите мне сумму на листочки, пожалуйста
napishyti mnye soomoo na listochki, pazhaloosta

can I pay by credit card?
я могу заплатить кредитной картой?
ya magoo zaplatit' kriditnaï kartaï?

I'll pay in cash
я заплачу наличными
ya zaplachyoo nalichnymi

I'm sorry, I haven't got any change
извините, но у меня нет мелочи
izviniti, no oo minya nyet myelachi

can I have a receipt?
могу я получить чек?
magoo ya paloochit' chek?

Understanding

платите в кассы
pay at the cash desk

как вы будете оплачивать?
kak vy booditi aplachivat'?
how would you like to pay?

у вас есть наша карточка?
oo vas yes't' nasha kartachka?
do you have a (loyalty) card?

у вас не будет помельче?
oo vas ni boodit pamyel'chi?
do you have anything smaller?

вот ваш чек и ваша сдача
vot vash chyek i vasha zdachya
here is your receipt and your change

у вас есть паспорт или документ, удостоверяющий личность?
oo vas yes't' paspart ili dakoomyent, oodastviryayooschi lichnas't'?
have you got a passport or any ID?

подпишите вот здесь, пожалуйста
patpishyti vot z'dyes', pazhaloosta
could you sign here, please?

FOOD

Expressing yourself

where can I buy food around here?
где здесь можно купить продукты?
gdye z'dyes' mozhna koopit' pradookty?

is there a market?
здесь есть рынок?
z'dyes' yes't' rynak?

is there a bakery near here?
здесь есть булочная?
z'dyes' yes't' boolachnaya?

I'm looking for muesli
где можно найти мюсли?
gdye mozhna naiti myoosli?

I'd like five slices of ham
пять кусков ветчины, пожалуйста
pyat' kooskof vichiny, pazhaloosta

could you weigh me a small piece of that cheese
взвесьте мне, пожалуйста, небольшой кусочек того сыра
vzvyes'ti mnye, pazhaloosta, nibal'shoï koosochik tavo syra

it's for four people
это на четверых
eta na chitviryH

about 300 grams
примерно триста грамм
primyerna trista gram

a kilo of apples, please
пожалуйста, килограмм яблок
pazhaloosta, kilagram yablak

a bit less/more
побольше/поменьше
pabol'she/pamyen'she

can I taste it?
я могу попробовать?
ya magoo paprobavat'?

does it travel well?
это можно взять в дорогу?
eta mozhna vzyat' v darogoo?

Understanding

колбасные изделия	sausage products
кондитерские изделия	confectionery products
молочные продукты	dairy products
полуфабрикат	semi-prepared foods
домашний	homemade
срок годности/годен до …	best before …
деликатесы	delicacies

рынок работает каждый день до часу дня
rynak rabotait kazhdy dyen' da chyasoo dnya
there's a market every day until 1pm

на углу есть магазин, он работает допоздна
na oogloo yes't' magazin, on rabotait dopazna
there's a grocer's just on the corner that's open late

CLOTHES

Expressing yourself

I'm looking for the menswear section
я ищу секцию мужской одежды
ya ischyoo syektsyyoo mooshskoï adyezhdy

no thanks, I'm just looking
нет, спасибо, я просто смотрю
nyet, spasiba, ya prosta smatryoo

can I try it on?
я могу это примерить?
ya magoo eta primyerit'?

I'd like to try the ... in the window
я хочу примерить ... с витрины
ya Hachyoo primyerit' ... s vitriny

I take a size 39 *(in shoes)*
я ношу тридцать девятый размер
ya nashoo tritsat' divyaty razmyer

where are the changing rooms?
где примерочные?
gdye primyerachnyye?

it doesn't fit
это мне не подошло
eta mnye ni padashlo

it's too big/small/loose/tight
это мне велико/мало/широко/узко
eta mnye viliko/malo/shyrako/oozka

do you have it in other colours?
у вас есть то же, но других цветов?
oo vas yes't' to zhe, no droogiH tsvitof?

do you have it in a smaller/bigger size?
у вас есть на размер больше/меньше?
oo vas yes't' na razmyer bol'she/myen'she?

do you have them in red?
у вас есть красного цвета?
oo vas yes't' krasnava tsvyeta?

yes, that's fine, I'll take it
да, это подошло, я это беру
da, eta padashlo, ya eta biroo

no, I don't like it
нет, мне не нравится
nyet, mnye ni nravitsa

I'll think about it
я пока подумаю
ya paka padoomayoo

I'd like to return this, it doesn't fit
я бы хотел (m)/хотела (f) вернуть эту вещь, она мне не подходит
ya by Hatyel/Hatyela virnoot' etoo vyesch', ona mnye ni patHodit

this has a hole in it, can I get a refund/exchange it?
здесь дырка, могу я вернуть деньги/обменять вещь?
z'dyes' dyrka, magoo ya virnoot' dyen'gi/abminyat' vyesch'?

Understanding

примерочные	changing rooms
одежда для детей	children's clothes
женская одежда	ladieswear
бельё	lingerie
мужская одежда	menswear
уценённый товар обмену и возврату не подлежит	sale items cannot be changed or returned

у нас есть только синего и чёрного цвета
oo nas yes't' tol'ka siniva i chyornava tsvyeta
we only have it in blue or black

этот размер у нас закончился
etat razmyer oo nas zakonchilsya
we don't have any left in that size

хотите это примерить?
Hatiti eta primyerit'
would you like to try it on?

вам идёт
vam idyot
it suits you

на вас хорошо сидит
na vas Harasho sidit
it's a good fit

вы сможете вернуть, если не подойдёт
vy smozhyti virnoot', yesli ni padaïdyot
you can bring it back if it doesn't fit

SOUVENIRS AND PRESENTS

Expressing yourself

I'm looking for a present to take home
я ищу подарок домой
ya ischyoo padarak damoï

what else could you suggest?
а что ещё вы можете мне посоветовать?
a shto ischyo vy mozhyti mnye pasavyetavat'?

could you gift-wrap it for me?
вы не могли бы завернуть в подарочную упаковку?
vy ni magli by zavirnoot' v padarachnooyoo oopakofkoo?

Understanding

100% дерево/серебро/золото/ шерсть	100% wood/silver/gold/wool
ручная работа	handmade
изделие народного промысла	traditionally made product

на какую сумму вы рассчитываете?
na kakooyoo soomoo vy raschityvaiti?
how much do you want to spend?

вы ищете подарок?
vy ischiti padarak?
is it for a present?

могу вам посоветовать матрёшку/самовар/платок/шапку
magoo vam pasavyetyvat' matryoshkoo/samovar/platok/shapkoo
I would recommend a matryoshka/samovar/shawl/fur hat

PHOTOS

The basics

black and white	чёрно-белый *chyorna byely*
batteries	батарейки *bataryeïki*
camera	фотоаппарат *fataaparat*
colour	цветной *tsvitnoï*
copy	отпечаток *atpichyatak*
digital camera	цифровой фотоаппарат *tsyfravoï fataaparat*
disposable camera	одноразовый фотоаппарат *adnarazavy fataaparat*
exposure	проявка *prayafka*
film	плёнка *plyonka*
flash	вспышка *fspyshka*
frame	рамка *ramka*
glossy paper	глянцевая бумага *glyantsyvaya boomaga*
matte paper	матовая бумага *matavaya boomaga*
memory card	карта памяти *karta pamyati*
negative	негатив *nigatif*
passport photo	фото на паспорт *fota na paspart*
photo album	фотоальбом *fotaal'bom*
photo booth	фотомагазин *fotamagazin*
reprint	перепечатывать *piripichyatyvat'*
size	размер *razmyer*
slide	кадр/снимок *kadr/snimak*
to get photos developed	проявить фотографии *prayavit' fatagrafii*
to take a photo/photos	снимать/фотографировать *snimat'/fatagrafiravat'*

Expressing yourself

could you take a photo of us, please?
вы можете нас сфотографировать?
vy mozhyti nas sfatagrafiravat'?

you just have to press this button
надо просто нажать на эту кнопку
nada prosta nazhat' na etoo knopkoo

I'd like a 200 ASA colour film
мне нужна плёнка с чувствительностью 200
mnye noozhna plyonka s chyustvitil'nast'yoo dvyes'ti

do you have black and white films?
у вас есть чёрно-белые плёнки?
oo vas yes't' chyorna-byelyye plyonki?

how much is it to develop a film of 36 photos?
сколько будет стоить проявка плёнки на 36 кадров?
skol'ka boodit stoit' prayafka plyonki na tritsat' shes't' kadraf?

when will the photos be ready?
когда будут готовы фотографии?
kagda boodoot gatovy fatagrafii?

I'd like to have this film developed
я хочу проявить эту плёнку
ya Hachyoo prayavit' etoo plyonkoo

three copies of this one and two of this one
три отпечатка этого кадра и два этого
tri atpichyatka etava kadra i dva etava

can I print my digital photos here?
вы печатаете цифровые фотографии?
vy pichyataiti tsyfravyi fatagrafii?

can you put these photos on a CD for me?
вы можете записать мне эти фотографии на диск?
vy mozhyti zapisat' mnye eti fatagrafii na disk?

I've come to pick up my photos
я хочу получить свой заказ
ya Hachyoo paloochit' svoi zakas

I've got a problem with my camera
у меня что-то случилось с фотоаппаратом
oo minya shto-ta sloochilas' s fataaparatam

the flash doesn't work
вспышка не работает
fspyshka ni rabotait

Understanding

проявка в течение часа	photos developed in one hour
цифровая печать фотографий	digital photos developed
моментальная печать	express service
запись фотографий на CD	photos copied onto CD

может быть, села батарейка
mozhyt byt', syela bataryeïka
maybe the battery's dead

у нас есть цифровой принтер
oo nas yes't' tsyfravoï printyr
we have a machine for printing digital photos

ьаше имя?
vashe imya?
what's your name, please?

когда вы хотите забрать фотографии?
kagda vy Hatiti zabrat' fatagrafii?
when do you want to collect the photos?

мы сможем проявить их в течение часа
my smozhym prayavit' iH f tichyenii chyasa
we can develop them in an hour

ваши фотографии будут готовы в четверг во второй половине дня
vashy fatagrafii boodoot gatovy f chitvyerk va ftaroï palavini dnya
your photos will be ready on Thursday afternoon

BANKS

ⓘ

Cash dispensers can be found at banks and in some hotels, but otherwise there are relatively few in Russia. For safety reasons, it's best to avoid withdrawing money in the street if you do see a machine. International credit cards are not accepted everywhere, so you should make sure you have enough cash on you.

You can change money at banks and official bureaux de change, but also in some shops and hotels. Because of the large number of counterfeit notes in Russia, never change money in the street even if you are offered a better exchange rate.

Banks are generally open Monday to Friday from 9am to 5 or 6pm.

The basics

bank	банк *bank*
bank account	(банковский) счёт *(bankafski) schyot*
banknote	купюра *koopyoora*
bureau de change	обменный пункт *abmyeny poonkt*
cash	наличные *nalichnyye*
cashpoint	банкомат *bankamat*
change	*(small change)* мелочь *myelach'; (money given back)* сдача *zdachya*
cheque	чек *chyek*
coin	монета *manyeta*
commission	комиссия *kamisiya*
credit card	кредитная карта *kriditnaya karta*
exchange rate	курс обмена *koors abmyena*
foreign currency	валюта *valyoota*
PIN (number)	PIN код, ПИН код *pin kot*
roubles	рубли *roobli*
transfer	перевод *pirivot*
Travellers Cheques®	дорожные чеки *darozhnyye chyeki*
withdrawal	снятие денег со счёта *snyatiye dyenyik sa schyota*

| **to change currency** | обменять валюту *abminyat' valyootoo* |
| **to withdraw** | снимать *snimat'* |

Expressing yourself

where I can get some money changed?
где я могу поменять деньги?
gdye ya magoo paminyat' dyen'gi?

are banks open on Saturdays?
банки работают по субботам?
banki rabotayoot pa soobotam?

I'm looking for a cashpoint
я ищу банкомат
ya ischyoo bankamat

I'd like to change £100
мне нужно обменять сто фунтов
mnye noozhna abminyat' sto foontaf

what commission do you charge?
какая у вас комиссия?
kakaya oo vas kamisiya?

I'd like to transfer some money
я хочу перевести деньги
ya Hachyoo pirivisti dyen'gi

I'd like to report the loss of my credit card
я хочу заявить о пропаже кредитной карты
ya Hachyoo zayavit' a prapazhe kriditnaï karty

the cashpoint has swallowed my card
банкомат проглотил мою карточку
bankamat praglatil mayoo kartachkoo

Understanding

| обмен валюты | currency exchange |

пожалуйста, вставьте ьашу карту
please insert your card

€

пожалуйста, введите PIN код
please enter your PIN number

пожалуйста, выберите необходимую сумму
please select the amount you require

распечатать чек?
withdrawal with receipt?

подождите, ваш запрос обрабатывается
please wait, your request is being processed

банкомат (временно) не работает
cashpoint (temporarily) out of service

Some informal expressions

бабки cash
быть при деньгах to be loaded
обменник exchange point
деревянные roubles
зелёные dollars
штука баксов 1,000 dollars
стольник 100 roubles/dollars/etc
полтинник 50 roubles/dollars/etc
десятка 10 roubles/dollars/etc

POST OFFICES

ⓘ

Post offices are generally open from 9am to 6 or 7pm. The central post office in Moscow is open 24 hours a day. Letter boxes are blue, with no separate slots for different destinations. Big hotels often have their own post offices where you can buy stamps and send letters and parcels. Major post offices may offer Internet access.

Addresses are written "upside down" in relation to the way we write them: the name of the country comes first along with the postcode, followed by the town, street name and house/apartment number, with the addressee's name at the bottom. The addressee's postcode is also written in the bottom left-hand corner.

Recently express post services run by companies such as DHL, EMS and Pony Express have offered an alternative to the slower, less reliable state postal service.

The basics

airmail	авиапочта *aviapochta*
envelope	конверт *kanvyert*
letter	письмо *pis'mo*
mail	почта *pochta*
parcel	посылка *pasylka*, бандероль *bandyrol'*
post	почта *pochta*
postbox	почтовый ящик *pachtovy yaschik*
postcard	открытка *atkrytka*
postcode	индекс *indeks*
poste restante	до востребования *da vastryebavaniya*
post office	почта *pochta*
registered letter	заказное письмо *zakaznoye pis'mo*
stamp	марка *marka*
telegram	телеграмма *tiligrama*
to post	посылать по почте *pasylat' pa pochti*
to send	посылать *pasylat'*
to write	писать *pisat'*

Expressing yourself

is there a post office around here?
где поблизости есть почта?
gdye pablizas'ti yes't' pochta?

is there a postbox near here?
здесь рядом есть почтовый ящик?
z'dyes' ryadam yes't' pachtovy yaschik?

is the post office open on Saturdays?
почта работает по субботам?
pochta rabotait pa soobotam?

what time does the post office close?
до которого часа работает почта?
da katorava chiasa rabotait pochta?

do you sell stamps?
у вас есть марки?
oo vas yes't' marki?

I'd like ... stamps for the UK, please
мне ... марок в Великобританию, пожалуйста
mnye ... marak v vilikabritaniyoo, pazhaloosta

where can I buy envelopes?
где можно купить конверты?
gdye mozhna koopit' kanvyerty?

how long will it take to arrive?
сколько времени это будет идти?
skol'ka vryemini eta boodit iti ?

Understanding

выемка писем производится с 8.30 до 9.00	collection between 8.30 and 9.00
не бросать	fragile
получатель	recipient
отправитель	sender

письмо идёт от трех до пяти дней
pis'mo idyot at tryoH da piti dneï
it'll take between three and five days

INTERNET CAFÉS AND E-MAIL

ⓘ

There are relatively few Internet cafés in Russia, except in the major cities. More Russians now have Internet access at home although it is rather expensive. The QWERTY keyboard is used in most Internet cafés. The name of the famous Internet café chain in Moscow is **Cafemax**.

The basics

at sign	собачка *sabachka*
e-mail	e-mail *i-meil*
e-mail address	электронный адрес *iliktrony adris*
Internet café	интернет-кафе *intyrnet-kafe*
key	клавиша *klavisha*
keyboard	клавиатура *klaviatoora*
to copy	копировать *kapiravat'*
to cut	вырезать *vyrizat'*
to delete	удалить *oodalit'*
to download	загрузить *zagroozit'*
to e-mail somebody	отправить кому-нибудь e-mail *atpravit' kamoo-niboot' i-meil*
to paste	вставить *fstavit'*
to receive	получить *paloochit'*
to save	сохранить *sakhranit'*
to send an e-mail	послать сообщение по e-mail'y *paslat' saapschyeniye pa i-meiloo*

Expressing yourself

is there an Internet café near here?
здесь есть поблизости интернет-кафе?
z'dyes' yes't' pablizas'ti intyrnet-kafe?

do you have an e-mail address?
у вас есть e-mail?
oo vas yes't' i-meil?

how do I get online?
как я могу выйти в Интернет?
kak ya magoo vyïti v internet?

I'd just like to check my e-mails
я просто хотел *(m)*/хотела *(f)* проверить почту
ya prosta Hatyel/Hatyela pravyerit' pochtoo

would you mind helping me, I'm not sure how it works
вы не могли бы мне помочь, я не знаю, как это работает
vy ni magli by mnye pamoch', ya ni znayoo, kak eta rabotait

I can't find the at sign on this keyboard
я не могу найти собачку на клавиатуре
ya ni magoo naïti sabachkoo na klaviatoori

something isn't working
тут что-то не работает
toot shto-ta ni rabotait

how much will it be for half an hour?
сколько стоит полчаса пользования Интернетом?
skol'ka stoit palchasa pol'zavaniya intyernetam?

when do I pay?
когда я должен заплатить?
kagda ya dolzhyn zaplatit'?

Understanding

пройдите за компьютер номер ...
praïditi za kamp'yutyr nomir...
go to computer number ...

вам придется подождать примерно двадцать минут
vam pridyotsa padazhdat' primyerna dvatsat' minoot
you'll have to wait for 20 minutes or so

если у вас что-то не получается, просто позовите мен
yesli oo vas shto-ta ni paloochyaitsa, prosta pazaviti minya
just ask if you're not sure what to do

у вас закончилось время
oo vas zakonchilas' vryemya
your time has run out

TELEPHONE

ⓘ

You should be able to use your mobile phone in Russia provided that it is enabled for international roaming. Alternatively, you can rent a mobile handset from most mobile phone companies in the country. The most popular networks are **МТС** (MTS *em-tee-es*), **БиЛайн** (Beeline *bilain*) and **Мегафон** (Megafon *migafon*).

Phone boxes usually take cards **телефонная карта** *(tilifonaya karta)*, which you can buy at the counters in metro stations. In Saint Petersburg, the phones in metro stations also take tokens **жетоны** *(zhytony)*.

To call the UK from Russia, dial 810 44 followed by the phone number, including the area code but omitting the first zero. To call Ireland, first dial 810 353, and for the US and Canada 810 1.

To call Russia from abroad, dial 007 followed by the area code (495 for Moscow, 812 for Saint Petersburg) and the seven-digit phone number.

The basics

answering machine	автоответчик *aftaatvyechik*
directory enquiries	справочная *spravachnaya*
hello	алло *alo*
international call	международный звонок *mizhdoonarodny zvanok*
local call	местный звонок *myesny zvanok*
message	сообщение *saapschyeniye*
mobile	мобильный телефон (мобильник) *mabil'ny tilifon*
national call	междугородный звонок *mizhdoogarodny zvanok*
phone	телефон *tilifon*
phone book	телефонная книга/телефонный справочник *tilifonaya kniga/tilifony spravachnik*
phone box	телефонная кабина/телефон-автомат *tilifonaya kabina/tilifon-aftamat*

phone call	телефонный звонок *tilifony zvanok*
phone number	номер телефона *nomir tilifona*
phonecard	телефонная карта *tilifonaya karta*
ringtone	звонок *zvanok*
telephone	телефон *tilifon*
Yellow Pages®	жёлтые страницы *zholtyye stranitsy*
to call somebody	звонить кому-нибудь *zvanit' kamoo-niboot'*
to dial	набирать номер *nabirat' nomir*

Expressing yourself

where can I buy a phonecard?
где я могу купить телефонную карту?
gdye ya magoo koopit' tilifonooyoo kartoo?

how much does it cost for a minute's call?
сколько стоит минута разговора?
skol'ka stoit minoota razgavora?

how do I call England?
как мне позвонить в Англию?
kak mnye pazvanit' v angliyoo?

is there a phone box near here, please?
где здесь поблизости телефон-автомат?
gdye z'dyes' pablizasti tilifon-aftamat?

can I recharge my mobile?
я могу здесь подзарядить мобильный телефон?
ya magoo z'dyes' padzaridit' mabil'ny tilifon?

do you have a mobile number?
у вас есть мобильный?
oo vas yes't' mabil'ny?

how can I contact you?
как можно с вами связаться?
kak mozhna s vami svizatsa?

did you get my message?
вы получили моё сообщение?
vy paloochili mayo saapschyenii?

Understanding

набранный вами номер не существует/неправильно набран номер
nabrany vami nomir ni sooschistvooit/nipravil'na nabran nomir
the number you have dialled has not been recognized

нажмите звёздочку/решётку
nazhmiti zvyozdachkoo/rishotkoo
please press the star/hash key

MAKING A CALL

Expressing yourself

hello, this is Dan Brown (speaking)
здравствуйте, это Дэн Браун
zdrastvooitye, eta den braoon

hello, could I speak to …, please?
здравствуйте, могу я поговорить с …?
zdrastvooitye, magoo ya pagavarit' s …?

hello, is that Nadia?
алло, это Надя?
alo, eta nadya?

do you speak English?
вы говорите по-английски?
vy gavariti pa-angliski

could you speak more slowly, please?
вы не могли бы говорить медленнее?
vy ni magli by gavarit' myedliniye?

I can't hear you, could you speak up, please?
я вас не слышу, говорите громче, пожалуйста
ya vas ni slyshoo, gavariti gromchi, pazhaloosta

could you tell him/her I called?
вы не могли бы передать ему/ей, чтоя звонил/звонила?
vy ni magli by piridat' yimoo/yeї, shto ya zvanil/zvanila?

could you ask him/her to call me back?
вы не могли бы попросить его/её перезвонить мне?
vy ni magli by paprasit' yivo/yiyo pirizvanit' mnye?

my name is ... and my number is ...
меня зовут ..., мой номер телефона ,,,
minya zavoul ..., mòi nomir tilifona ...

do you know when he/she might be available?
а вы не знаете, когда его/её можно застать?
a vy ni znaiti, kagda yivo/yiyo mozhna zastat'?

I'll call back later
я перезвоню позже
ya pirizvanyoo pozhe

thank you, goodbye
спасибо, до свидания
spasiba, da svidaniya

Understanding

кто его/её спрашивает?
kto yivo/yiyo sprashyvait?
who's asking for him/her?

вы не туда попали
vy ni tooda papali
you've got the wrong number

его/её сейчас нет
yivo/yiyo sichyas nyet
he's/she's not here at the moment

ему что-нибудь передать?
yimoo shto-niboot' piridat'?
do you want to leave a message?

я передам ему/ей, что вы звонили
ya piridam yimoo/yeï, shto vy zvanili
I'll tell him/her you called

я скажу, чтобы он/она вам перезвонил/перезвонила
ya skazhoo, shtoby on/ana vam pirizvanil/pirizvanila
I'll ask him/her to call you back

оставайтесь на линии
astavaïtis' na linii
stay on the line

сейчас я передам ему/ей трубку
sichyas ya piridam yimoo/yeï troopkoo
I'll just pass you over to him/her

PROBLEMS

Expressing yourself

I don't know the code
я не знаю код
ya ni znayoo kot

it's engaged
занято
zanyata

there's no reply
никто не подходит
nikto ni patHodit

I couldn't get through
я не могу дозвониться
ya ni magoo dazvanitsa

I don't have much credit left on my phone
у меня недостаточно денег на телефоне
oo minya nidastatachna dyenik na tilifoni

we're about to get cut off
нас сейчас разъединят
nas sichyas raz-yidinyat

the reception's really bad
связь очень плохая
svyas' ochin' plaHaya

I can't get a signal
здесь плохой приём
z'des' plaHoï priyom

Understanding

я вас не слышу
ya vas ni slyshoo
I can hardly hear you

нас разъединили
nas raz-yidinili
we were cut off

перезвоните, пожалуйста
pirizvaniti, pazhaloosta
please call back

абонент временно недоступен
abonyent vryemina nidastoopin
the number is temporarily unavailable

Common abbreviations
раб. тел. = рабочий телефон *rabochi tilifon* work number
дом. тел. = домашний телефон *damashni tilifon* home number
моб. тел. = мобильный телефон *mabil'ny tilifon* mobile number

---

Some informal expressions
мобильник здесь плохо ловит/совсем не
ловит there's no signal here
он повесил трубку he hung up on me
звякнуть to call somebody
скинь мне СМСку send me a text

To get a visa, you must be able to prove you have appropriate health insurance. EU nationals do not need any vaccination certificates, but anyone wishing to stay longer than three months must produce an HIV-negative certificate.

Antibiotics can be bought over the counter in Russia. Medicines are sold in pharmacies **аптека** *(aptyeka)* and at specially licensed kiosks in some metro stations. There is an emergency pharmacy known as *dizhoornaya aptyeka* in every neighbourhood. Be warned that some medicines are not available in Russia, so it's best to stock up before you go, particularly if you are on any kind of regular medication.

Check the sell-by dates on food, particularly frozen goods.

In a medical emergency, call **03** for an ambulance.

The basics

allergy	аллергия *alirgiya*
ambulance	скорая помощь *skoraya pomasch'*
analysis	анализ *analis*
aspirin	аспирин *aspirin*
blood	кровь *krof'*
broken	сломан *sloman*
casualty (department)	приёмное отделение *priyomnaye atdilyeniye*
chemist's	аптека *aptyeka*
condom	презерватив *prizirvatif*
dentist	стоматолог *stamatolak*
diarrhoea	понос *panos*
doctor	доктор *doktar*
food poisoning	пищевое отравление *pischivoye atravlyeniye*
GP	терапевт *tyrapyeft*
gynaecologist	гинеколог *ginikolak*
health centre	поликлиника *paliklinika*

hospital	больница *bal'nitsa*
infection	инфекция *infyektsyya*
medicine	лекарство *likarstva*
operation	операция *apiratsyya*
painkiller	обезболивающее *abizbolivayooschiye*
periods	месячные *myesichnyi*
plaster	пластырь *plastyr'*
rash	сыпь *syp'*
spot	прыщ *prysch*
surgical spirit	медицинский спирт *miditsynski spirt*
tablet	таблетка *tablyetka*
temperature	температура *timpiratoora*
vaccination	прививка *privifka*
x-ray	рентген *ringyen*
to disinfect	дезинфицировать *dizinfitsyravat'*
to faint	обморок *obmarak*
to vomit	рвота *rvota*

Expressing yourself

does anyone have an aspirin/a plaster, by any chance?
ни у кого случайно нет аспирина/пластыря?
ni oo kavo sloochyaïna nyet aspirina/plastyrya?

I need to see a doctor
мне нужен врач
mnye noozhyn vrach

where can I find a doctor?
где я могу найти врача?
gdye ya magoo naïti vrachya?

I'd like to make an appointment for today
я хочу записаться на приём на сегодня
ya Hachyoo zapisatsa na priyom na sivodnya

as soon as possible
как можно раньше
kak mozhna ran'she

can you send an ambulance to …
пришлите, пожалуйста, скорую помощь по адресу …
prishliti, pazhaloosta, skorooyoo pomasch pa adrisoo …

I've broken my glasses
я разбил (m)/разбила (f) очки
ya razbil/razbila achki

I've lost a contact lens
я потерял (m)/потеряла (f) линзы
ya patiryal/patiryala linzy

Understanding

приёмное отделение	casualty department
рецепт	prescription
травмпункт	doctor's surgery

до четверга всё занято
da chitvirga fsyo zanita
there are no available appointments until Thursday

в пятницу, в два часа вам подойдёт?
f pyatnitsoo vyechiram vam padaidyot?
is Friday at 2pm OK?

AT THE DOCTOR'S OR THE HOSPITAL

Expressing yourself

I have an appointment with Dr ...
мне назначено к доктору ...
mne naznachina k doktaroo ...

I don't feel very well
я плохо себя чувствую
ya ploHa sibya choostvooyoo

I feel very weak
у меня сильная слабость
oo minya sil'naya slabas't'

I don't know what it is
я не знаю, что со мной
ya ni znayoo, shto sa mnoï

I've got a headache
у меня болит голова
oo minya balit galava

I've been bitten/stung by ...
меня укусил (m)/укусила (f)/ужалил (m)/ужалила (f) ...
minya ookoosil/ookoosila/oozhalil/oozhalila ...

I've got toothache/stomachache
у меня болит зуб/живот
oo minya balit zoop/zhyvot

I've got a sore throat
у меня болит горло
oo minya balit gorla

my back hurts
у меня болит спина
oo minya balit spina

it hurts here
у меня болит здесь
oo minya balit z'dyes'

I feel sick
меня тошнит
minya tashnit

it's got worse
стало ещё хуже
stala ischyo Hoozhe

it's been three days
это продолжается уже три дня
eta pradalzhaitsa oozhe tri dnya

it's never happened to me before
раньше со мной такого не было
ran'she sa mnoï takova nye byla

it started last night
это началось прошлой ночью
eta nachilos' proshloï noch'yoo

I've got a temperature
у меня температура
oo minya timpiratoora

I have asthma
у меня астма
oo minya astma

I have a heart condition
у меня больное сердце
oo minya bal'noye syertse

I've been on antibiotics for a week and I'm not getting any better
я неделю пью антибиотики, но лучше не становится
ya nidyelyoo p'yoo antibiotiki, no lootshe ni stanovitsa

it itches
здесь чешется
z'dyes' chyeshetsa

I'm on the pill
я пью противозачаточные таблетки
ya p'yoo protivazachatachnyye tablyetki

I'm four months pregnant
я на четвёртом месяце беременности
ya na chitvyortam myesitsy biryeminasti

I'm allergic to penicillin
у меня аллергия на пенициллин
oo minya alirgiya na pinitsylin

I fell and hurt my back
я упал (m)/упала (f) и ушиб (m)/ушибла (f) спину
ya oopul/oopula i ooshyp/ooshybla spinoo

I've had a blackout
я потерял (m)/потеряла (f) сознание
ya patiryal/patiryala saznanii

I've lost a filling
у меня выпала пломба
oo minya vypala plomba

I have a burn
у меня ожог
oo minya azhok

is it serious?
это серьёзно?
eta sir'yozna?

is it contagious?
это заразно?
eta zarazna?

how is he/she?
как он/она?
kak on/ana?

how much do I owe you?
сколько я вам должен (m)/должна (f)?
skol'ka ya vam dolzhyn/dalzhna?

Understanding

подождите, пожалуйста в приёмной
padazhditi, pazhaloosta f priyomnai
if you'd like to take a seat in the waiting room

на что жалуетесь?/что у вас болит?
na shto zhalooitis'?/shto oo vas balit?
where does it hurt?

сделайте глубокий вздох
z'dyelaiti goolboki vzdoH
take a deep breath

разденьтесь, пожалуйста
raz'dyen'tis', pazhaloosta
could you get undressed, please?

пожалуйста, откройте рот
pazhaloosta, atkroiti rot
open your mouth, please

ложитесь, пожалуйтесь
lazhytis', pazhaloosta
lie down, please

больно, когда я здесь нажимаю?
bol'na, kagda ya z'dyes' nazhymayoo?
does it hurt when I press here?

вы делали прививку от …?
vy dyelali privifkoo at…?
have you been vaccinated against …?

у вас есть аллергия на …?
oo vas yes't' alirgiya na…?
are you allergic to …?

вы принимаете другие лекарства?
vy prinimaiti droogii likarstva?
are you taking any other medication?

я выпишу вам рецепт
ya vypishoo vam ritsept
I'm going to write you a prescription

это быстро заживёт
eta bystra zazhyvyot
it should heal quickly

вам нужна операция
vam noozhna apiratsyya
you're going to need an operation

приходите ко мне через неделю
priHaditi ka mnye chiriz nidyelyoo
come and see me in a week

AT THE CHEMIST'S

Expressing yourself

I'd like a box of plasters, please
упаковку пластыря, пожалуйста
oopakofkoo plastyrya, pazhaloosta

could I have something for a bad cold/cough/headache?
у вас есть что-нибудь от простуды/кашля/головной боли?
oo vas yes't' shto-niboot' at prastoody/kashlya/galavnoï boli?

I'm allergic to aspirin
у меня аллергия на аспирин
oo minya alirgiya na aspirin

⊕

how should I take this medicine?
как принимать это лекарство?
kak prinimat' eta likarstva?

I'd like a bottle of solution for contact lenses
мне нужен раствор для контактных линз
mnye noozyn rastvor dlya kantaktnyH lins

Understanding

капсула	capsule
мазь	ointment
микстура	syrup
отпускается только по рецепту	available on prescription only
побочные действия	possible side-effects
порошок	powder
принимать три раза в день перед едой/после еды	take three times a day before meals/ after meals
противопоказания	contra-indications
свечи	suppositories
сироп	syrup
таблетка	tablet

Some informal expressions

я слёг/слегла to be stuck in bed
я подхватил жуткий грипп I've an awful dose of flu
у меня течет из носа I've got a runny nose
отключиться to pass out

HEALTH

PROBLEMS AND EMERGENCIES

If you get lost in a town, you can ask for directions at the reception desk of a hotel. You can also ask a traffic policeman; you can find them at busy junctions where their duties include directing traffic and recording the details of road accidents. For lost property, ask for the **бюро находок** *(byooro naHodak)*. The emergency numbers are **01** for the fire brigade, **02** for the police and **03** for an ambulance. **09** can be used for directory enquiries.

The basics

accident	несчастный случай *nischyasny sloochii*
ambulance	скорая помощь *skoraya pomasch*
broken	сломан *(m)*/сломана *(f) sloman/slomana*
disabled	инвалид *invalit*
doctor	врач *vrach*
emergency	срочность *srochnast'*
fire brigade	пожарные *pazharnyye*
fire	пожар *pazhar*
hospital	больница *bal'nitsa*
ill	болен *(m)*/больна *(f) bolin/bal'na*
injured	ранен *(m)*/ранена *(f) ranin/ranina*
injury	травма *travma*
police	милиция *militsyya*
traffic police	ГАИ *gai*

Expressing yourself

can you help me?
вы можете мне помочь?
vy mozhyti mnye pamoch?

help!
помогите!
pamagiti!

fire!
пожар!
pazhar!

be careful!
осторожно!
astarozhna!

send for a doctor!
вызовите врача!
vyzaviti vrachya!

there's been an accident
произошёл несчастный случай
praizashol nischyasny sloochaii

could I borrow your phone, please?
можно позвонить с Вашего телефона?
mozhna pazvanit' s vashyva tilifona?

does anyone here speak English?
кто-нибудь говорит по-английски?
kto-niboot' gavarit pa-angliski?

I need to contact the British embassy/consulate
мне нужно связаться с британским посольством/консульством
mnye noozhna svizatsa s britanskim pasol'stvam/konsool'stvam

where's the nearest police station?
где ближайшее отделение милиции?
gdye blizhaïshye adilyeniye militsyi

what should I do?
что мне делать?
shto mnye dyelat'?

my bag's been snatched
у меня вырвали сумку
oo minya vyrvali soomkoo

my passport/credit card has been stolen
у меня украли паспорт/кредитную карту
oo minya ookrali paspart/kriditnooyoo kartoo

I've lost …
я потерял (m)/потеряла (f) …
ya patiryal/patiryala …

I've been attacked
на меня напали
na minya napali

my son/daughter is missing
мой сын/моя дочка потерялся/потерялась
moï syn/maya dochka patiryalsya/patiryalas'

my car's been towed away
у меня угнали машину
oo minya oognali mashynoo

I've broken down
у меня сломалась машина
oo minya slamalas' mashyna

there's a man following me
меня кто-то преследует
minya kto-ta prislyedooit

is there disabled access?
есть ли вход для инвалидов?
yes't' li fHot dlya invalidaf?

can you keep an eye on my things for a minute?
вы можете ненадолго присмотреть за моими вещами?
vy mozhyti ninadolga prismatryet' za maimi vischyami?

he's drowning, get help!
он тонет, помогите!
on tonit, pamagiti!

leave me alone
оставьте меня в покое
astaf'ti minya v pakoi

I'll call the police
я позову милицию
ya pazavoo militsyyoo

Understanding

аварийный выход	emergency exit
автосервис	breakdown service
бюро находок	lost property
не работает	out of order
осторожно, злая собака	beware of the dog
спасатели	mountain rescue
штраф 100 рублей	100-rouble fine

POLICE

Expressing yourself

I want to report something stolen
я хочу заявить о краже
ya Hachyoo zayavit' a krazhy

I need a document from the police for my insurance company
мне нужна справка из милиции для страховой компании
mnye noozhna sprafka iz militsyi dlya straHavoï kampanii

Understanding

Filling in forms

фамилия	surname
имя	first name
адрес	address
индекс	postcode
телефон	telephone
страна	country
национальность	nationality
число/месяц/год рождения	date/month/year of birth
место рождения	place of birth
возраст	age
пол	sex
семейное положение	marital status
цель визита	purpose of visit
длительность пребывания	duration of stay
дата прибытия/отъезда	arrival/departure date
место работы	place of work
серия и номер паспорта	passport number

откройте, пожалуйста, эту сумку
atkroïti, pazhaloosta, etoo soomkoo
would you open this bag, please?

что-нибудь пропало?
shto-niboot' prapala?
is something missing?

когда это произошло?
kagda eta praizashlo?
when did this happen?

где вы остановились?
gdye vy astanavilis'?
where were you staying?

вы можете его/ её описать?
vy mozhyti yivo/yiyo apisat'?
can you describe him/her/it?

заполните, пожалуйста, этот бланк
zapolniti, pazhaloosta, etat blank
would you fill in this form, please?

подпишите вот здесь, пожалуйста
patpishyti vot z'dyes', pazhaloosta
would you sign here, please?

TIME AND DATE

The basics

after	после *posli*
already	уже *oozhe*
always	всегда *fsigda*
at lunchtime	в обеденный перерыв *v abyediny piriryf*
at the beginning/end of	в начале/в конце *v nachyali/f kantse*
at the moment	сейчас *sichyas*
before	до *do*
between ... and ...	между ... и ... *myezhdoo ... i ...*
day	день *dyen'*
during	во время *va vryemya*
early	рано *rana*
evening	вечер *vyechir*
for a long time	долгое время *dolgaye vryemya*
from ... to ...	от ... до ... *ot ... do ...*
from time to time	время от времени *vryemya at vryemini*
in a little while	через какое-то время *chiris kakoye-ta vryemya*
in the evening	вечером *vyechiram*
in the middle of	в середине *f siridini*
last	прошлый *proshly*
late	поздно/с опозданием *pozna/s apazdaniyem*
midday	полдень *poldin'*
midnight	полночь *polnach*
morning	утро *ootra*
month	месяц *myesits*
never	никогда *nikagda*
next	следующий *slyedooschi*
night	ночь *noch*
not yet	ещё нет *ischyo nyet*
now	сейчас *sichyas*
occasionally	иногда *inagda*
often	часто *chyasta*
rarely	редко *ryetka*
recently	недавно *nidavna*

since	с тех пор *s tyeH por*
sometimes	иногда *inagda*
soon	скоро *skora*
still	всё ещё *fsyo ischyo*
straightaway	сразу/немедленно *srazoo/nimyedlina*
until	до тех пор, пока *da tyeH por, paka*
week	неделя *nidyelya*
weekend	выходные *vyHadnyi*
year	год *got*

see you soon!
до скорого!
da skorava!

see you later!
увидимся!/пока!/счастливо!
oovidimsya!/paka!/schisliva!

see you on Monday!
до понедельника!
da panidyel'nika!

have a good weekend!
хороших вам/тебе выходных!
HaroshyH vam/tibye vyHadnyH!

sorry I'm late
простите, я опоздал *(m)*/опоздала *(f)*
prastiti, ya apazdal/apazdala

I've got plenty of time
у меня много времени
oo minya mnoga vryemini

I'm in a rush
я тороплюсь
ya taraplyoos'

hurry up!
поторопись! *(sg)*/поторопитесь! *(pl)*
patarapis'!/patarapitis'!

just a minute, please
ещё минуту, пожалуйста!
ischyo minootoo, pazhaloosta

I had a late night
я вчера поздно лёг *(m)*/легла *(f)*
ya fchira pozna lyok/ligla

I waited ages
я ждал *(m)*/ждала *(f)* целую вечность
ya zhdal/zhdala tselooyoo vyechnas't'

I have to get up very early tomorrow to catch my plane
завтра мне надо встать очень рано, чтобы успеть на самолёт
zaftra mnye nada fstat' ochin' rana, shtoby oospyet' na samalyot

TIME AND DATE

we only have four days left
у нас осталось только четыре дня
oo nas astalas' tol'ka chityri dnya

THE DATE

How to express the date

To answer the question "what's the date today?", the ordinal number (1st, 2nd, 3rd etc) in the nominative case (see Grammar section) is used followed by the month and year in the genitive: **сегодня 10-ое сентября 2007-ого года** it's 10 September 2007 ("the tenth (day) of September of the year 2007").

To answer the question "when?", the ordinal number in the genitive is used followed by the month and year in the genitive: **2-ого января 2007-ого года** I'll see you on 2 January 2007.

To give the month or year, the preposition **в** is used followed by the prepositional case: in June 1867 **в июне 1867-ого года.**

To say that something happened between two dates, the preposition **между** is used followed by the ordinal number in the instrumental case: between 1904 and 1909 **между 1904-ым и 1909-ым годом.**

To give the century, the preposition **в** is used followed by the ordinal number and the century in the prepositional:

in the first century BC	в первом веке до н.э. (нашей эры)
in the third century BC	в третьем веке н.э
19th-century art	искусство девятнадцатого века
in the early/mid-20th century	в начале/середине двадцатого века
at the end of the 20th century	в конце двадцатого века

The basics

... ago	... назад ... *nazat*
at the beginning/end of	в начале/в конце *v nachali/f kantse*
in the middle of	в середине *v siridini*
in two days' time	через два дня *chiris dva dnya*

last night	прошлой ночью *proshlaï noch'yoo*
the day after tomorrow	послезавтра *poslizaftra*
the day before yesterday	позавчера *pazafchira*
today	сегодня *sivodnya*
tomorrow	завтра *zaftra*
tomorrow morning/afternoon/ evening	завтра утром/днём/вечером *zaftra ootram/dnyom/vyechiram*
yesterday	вчера *fchira*
yesterday morning/afternoon/ evening	вчера утром/днём/вечером *fchira ootram/dnyom/vyechiram*

Expressing yourself

I was born in 1975
я родился *(m)*/родилась *(f)* в тысяча девятьсот семьдесят пятом году
ya radilsya/radilas' f tysichya divitsot syemdisyat pyatam gadoo

I came here a few years ago
я приехал *(m)*/приехала *(f)* сюда несколько лет назад
ya priyeHal/priyeHala syooda neskal'ka lyet nazat

I spent a month in France last summer
прошлым летом я на месяц ездил *(m)*/ездила *(f)* во Францию
proshlym lyetam ya na myesits yez'dil/yez'dila va frantsyyoo

what's the date today?
какое сегодня число?
kakoye sivodnya chislo?

what day is it today?
какой сегодня день недели?
kakoï sivodnya dyen' nidyeli?

it's the 1st of May
сегодня первое мая
sivodnya pyervaye maya

I'm staying until Sunday
я здесь до воскресения
ya z'dyes' da vaskrisyen'ya

we're leaving tomorrow
мы завтра уезжаем
my zaftra ooizhaim

I already have plans for Tuesday
у меня уже есть планы на вторник
oo minya oozhe yes't' plany na ftornik

Understanding

каждый день	every day
на будущей неделе/в будущем году	next week/next year
однажды/дважды	once/twice
по будням/по выходным	on weekdays/weekends
по понедельникам	every Monday
с понедельника по пятницу	from Monday to Friday
три раза в день	three times a day

дом был построен в середине девятнадцатого века
dom byl pastroin f siridini divitnatsatava vyeka
the house was built in the mid-nineteenth century

летом здесь много народу
lyetam z'dyes' mnoga narodoo
it gets very busy here in the summer

когда вы уезжаете?
kagda vy ooizhaiti?
when are you leaving?

на сколько вы приехали?
na skol'ka vi priyeHali?
how long are you staying?

THE TIME

When telling the time, the cardinal number (1, 2, 3 etc) is used in the nominative case followed by the word **час** (hour) in the correct form (see the Numbers chapter), for example:

сейчас десять часов утра it's ten o'clock in the morning
сейчас четыре часа дня it's four o'clock in the afternoon
сейчас шесть часов вечера it's six o'clock in the evening

The basics

| half an hour | полчаса *polchisa* |
| in the afternoon | во второй половине дня *va ftaroï palavini dnya* |

in the morning	утром *ootram*
on time	вовремя *vovrimya*
quarter of an hour	пятнадцать минут *pitnatsat' minoot*
three quarters of an hour	сорок пять минут *sorak pyat' minoot*

Expressing yourself

excuse me, have you got the time, please?
вы не подскажете, который час?
vy ni patskazhyti, katory chyas?

what time is it?
который час?
katory chyas?

my watch is fast/slow
мои часы спешат/отстают
mai chisy spishat/atstayoot

it's exactly three o'clock
ровно три часа
rovna tri chisa

it's nearly one o'clock
почти час дня
pachti chyas dnya

it's ten past one
десять минут второго
dyesit' minoot ftarova

it's a quarter past one
час пятнадцать
chyas pitnatsat'

it's a quarter to one
без пятнадцати час
biz pitnatsati chyas

it's twenty past twelve
двадцать минут первого
dvatsat' minoot pyervava

it's twenty to twelve
без двадцати двенадцать
biz dvatsati dvinatsat'

it's half past one
половина второго/ час тридцать
palavina ftarova/chyas tritsat'

I arrived at about two o'clock
я приехал (m)/я приехала (f) где-то в три часа
ya priyeHal/a gdye-ta v tri chisa

I set my alarm for nine
я поставила будильник на девять
ya pastavila boodil'nik na dyevit'

I waited twenty minutes
я ждал (m)/ждала (f) двадцать минут
ya zhdal/a dvatsat' minoot

the train was fifteen minutes late
поезд опоздал на пятнадцать минут
poist apazdal na pitnatsat' minoot

I got home an hour ago
я вернулся *(m)*/вернулась *(f)* домой час назад
ya vyirnoolsya/vyirnoolas' damoï chyas nazat

shall we meet in half an hour?
давай встретимся через полчаса
davaï fstryetimsya chiris polchisa

I'll be back in a quarter of an hour
я вернусь через пятнадцать минут
ya vyirnoos' chiris pitnatsat' minoot

Understanding

отправление каждый час/ каждые полчаса	departs on the hour/on the half-hour
открыто с 10 до 16 без перерыва	open from 10am to 4pm without a break

я не знаю, который час
ya ni znayoo, katory chyas
I don't know what time it is

каждый вечер в семь часов
kazhdy vyechir, f syem' chisof
every evening at seven

магазин открывается в десять утра
magazin atkryvaitsa v dyesit' ootra
the shop opens at ten in the morning

> ### Some informal expressions
> **в час по чайной ложке** really slowly
> **у нас уйма/куча времени** we've got masses of time

(i)

Sums of money are written as follows: **150 руб.34 коп.** (150 roubles and 34 kopecks), pronounced *sto pit'disyat rooblyeï tritsat' chityri kapyeïki*.

On till receipts, a full stop is used for decimals as in English, for example 1352.45 (**тысяча триста пятьдесят два сорок пять** *tysicha trista pid'disyat dva sorak pyat'*). There is no need to say the words "roubles" or "kopecks".

0	ноль *nol'*
1	один *adin*
2	два *dva*
3	три *tri*
4	четыре *chityri*
5	пять *pyat'*
6	шесть *shes't*
7	семь *syem'*
8	восемь *vosim'*
9	девять *dyevit'*
10	десять *dyesit'*
11	одиннадцать *adinatsat'*
12	двенадцать *dvinatsat'*
13	тринадцать *trinatsat'*
14	четырнадцать *chityrnatsat'*
15	пятнадцать *pitnatsat'*
16	шестнадцать *shysnatsat'*
17	семнадцать *simnatsat'*
18	восемнадцать *vasimnatsat'*
19	девятнадцать *divitnatsat'*
20	двадцать *dvatsat'*
21	двадцать один *dvatsat' adin*
22	двадцать два *dvatsat' dva*
30	тридцать *tritsat'*
35	тридцать пять *tritsat' pyat'*
40	сорок *sorak*
50	пятьдесят *pid'disyat*

60	шестьдесят *shyz'disyat*
70	семьдесят *syemdisyat*
80	восемьдесят *vosimdisyat*
90	девяносто *divinosta*
100	сто *sto*
101	сто один *sto adin*
200	двести *dvyes'ti*
500	пятьсот *pitsot*
1000	тысяча *tysicha*
2000	две тысячи *dvye tysichi*
5000	пять тысяч *pyat' tysich*
10000	десять тысяч *dyesit' tysich*
1000000	миллион *milion*
first	первый *pyervy*
second	второй *ftaroï*
third	третий *tryeti*
fourth	четвёртый *chitvyorty*
fifth	пятый *pyaty*
sixth	шестой *shystoï*
seventh	седьмой *sid'moï*
eighth	восьмой *vas'moï*
ninth	девятый *divyaty*
tenth	десятый *disyaty*
twentieth	двадцатый *dvatsaty*

20 plus 3 equals 23
двадцать плюс три равно двадцать три
dvatsat' plyoos tri ravno dvatsat' tri

20 minus 3 equals 17
двадцать минус три равно семнадцать
dvatsat' minoos tri ravno simnatsat'

20 multiplied by 4 equals 80
двадцать умножить на четыре равно восемьдесят
dvatsat' oomnozhyt' na chityri ravno vosimdisyat

20 divided by 4 equals 5
двадцать разделить на четыре равно пять
dvatsat' raz'dilit' na chityri ravno pyat'

DICTIONARY

ENGLISH-RUSSIAN

Note: verbs are presented where necessary in imperfective/perfective pairs, eg **мочь/ смочь**. Adjectives are shown in their masculine singular form.

a (indefinite article) (see grammar)
able: to be able to мочь/смочь
  moch'/smoch'
about вокруг *vakrook*; **to be about
  to do** быть готовым сделать *byt'
  gatovym z'dyelat'*
above над *nad*, выше *vyshe*
abroad: to live abroad жить за
  границей *zhyt' za granitseï*; **to go
  abroad** ездить за границу *yez'dit'
  za granitsoo*
accept принимать/принять *prinimat'/
  prinyat'*
access доступ (m) *dostoop* **111**
accident несчастный случай (m)
  nischyasny sloochii **32, 110**
accommodation жильё (n) *zhyl'yo*
across через *chiris*
adaptor адаптер (m) *adaptyr*
address адрес (m) *adris*
admission входной билет (m)
  fHadnoï bilyet
advance: in advance заранее
  zaraniye
advice совет (m) *savyet*; **to ask
  someone's advice** просить совета
  prasit' savyeta
advise советовать/посоветовать
  savyetyvat'/pasavyetyvat'
aeroplane самолёт (m) *samalyot*
after после *posli*
afternoon вторая половина дня (f)
  ftaraya palavina dnya

aftersun (cream) крем после загара
  (m) *kryem posli zagara*
again снова *snova*, опять *apyat'*
against против *protif*
age возраст (m) *vozrast*
air воздух (m) *vozdooH*
air conditioning кондиционер (m)
  kanditsy-anyer
airline авиалиния (f) *avialiniya*
airmail авиапочта (f) *aviapochta*
airport аэропорт (m) *ayraport*
alarm clock будильник (m)
  boodil'nik
alcohol алкоголь (m) *alkagol'*
alive живой *zhyvoï*
all весь (m) *vyes*, вся (f) *fsya*, всё (n)
  fsyo, все (pl) *fsye*; **all day** целый день
  tsely' dyen'; **all week** всю неделю
  fsyoo nidyelyoo; **all the better** тем
  лучше *tyem lootshe*; **all the same** всё
  равно *fsyo ravno*; **all the time** всё
  время *fsyo vryemya*; **all inclusive** всё
  включено *fsyo fklyoochino*
allergic аллергический *alirgichiski* **47,
  105, 107**
almost почти *pachti*
already уже *oozhe*
also тоже *tozhe*, также *takzhe*
although хотя *Hatya*, тем не менее
  tyem ni myeniye
always всегда *fsigda*
ambulance скорая помощь (f)
  skoraya pomasch **103**
American (adj) американский
  amirikanski

American (noun) американец (m) *amirikanits*, американка (f) *amirikanka*

among среди *sridi*

anaesthetic обезболивающее (n) *abizbolivayoosheeye*

and и *i*

animal животное (n) *zhyvotnaye*

ankle лодыжка (f) *ladyshka*

anniversary юбилей (m) *yoobilyeї*, годовщина (f) *gadafshchina*

another другой *droogoï*

answer (noun) ответ (m) *atvyet*

answer (v) отвечать/ответить *atvichyat'/atvyetit'*

answering machine автоответчик (m) *aftaatvyechik*

ant муравей (m) *mooravyeï*

antibiotics антибиотик (m) *antibiotik*

anybody, anyone кто-нибудь *kto-niboot'*

anything что-нибудь *shto-niboot'*

anyway в любом случае *v lyoobom sloochii*

appendicitis аппендицит (m) *apinditsyt*

appointment свидание (n) *svidaniye*; **to make an appointment** назначать/назначить свидание *naznachat'/naznachit' svidaniye* **103**; **to have an appointment with** встречаться с (+ inst.) *fstrichyatsa s* **104**

April апрель (m) *apryel'*

area район (m) *raïon*; **in the area** в районе *v raïoni*

arm рука (f) *rooka*

around вокруг *vakrook*

arrange договариваться/договориться *dagavarivatsa/dagavaritsa*; **to arrange to meet** договариваться/договориться о встрече *dagavarivatsa/dagavaritsa a fstryechi*

arrival приезд (m) *priyest*

arrive приезжать/приехать *priyizzhat'/priyeHat'*

art искусство (n) *iskoostva*

artist художник (m) *Hoodozhnik*

as как *kak*; **as soon as possible** как можно раньше *kak mozhna ran'she*; **as soon as** не позже *ni pozzhe*; **as well as** также, как *tagzhe, kak*

ashtray пепельница (f) *pyepil'nitsa* **46**

ask спрашивать/спросить *sprashyvat'/sprasit'*; **to ask a question** задать вопрос *zadat' vapros*

aspirin аспирин (m) *aspirin*

asthma астма (f) *astma*

at в *v*, на *na*

attack (v) нападать/напасть *napadat'/napas't'* **110**

August август (m) *avgoost*

aunt тётя (f) *tyotya*

autumn осень (f) *osin'*

available доступный *dastoopny*, в наличии *v nalichii*

avenue проспект (m) *praspyekt*

away: 10 kilometres away на расстоянии 10 километров *na rasstayanii 10 kilamyetraf*

В

baby ребёнок (m) *ribyonak*

baby's bottle детская бутылочка (m) *dyetskaya bootylachka*

back спина *spina*; **at the back of** позади *pazadi*

backpack рюкзак (m) *ryoogzak*

bad плохой *plaHoï*; **it's not bad** неплохо *niploHa*

bag сумка (f) *soomka*

baggage багаж (m) *bagash*

bake печь *pyech'*

bakery булочная (f) *boolachnaya*

balcony балкон (m) *balkon*

bandage бинт (m) *bint*

bank банк (m) *bank* **91**

banknote купюра (f) *koopyoora*

bar бар (m) *bar*

barbecue барбекю (n) *barbikyoo*, шашлык (m) *shashlyk*

bath ванна (f) *vana*; **to have a bath** принимать ванну *prinimat' vanoo*
bathroom ванная (f) *vanaya*
bath towel банное полотенце (n) *banoye palatyentse*
battery батарея (f) *bataryeya*
be быть *byt'*
beard борода (f) *barada*
beautiful красивый *krasivy*
because потому что *patamoo shta*; **because of** из-за *iz-za*
bed кровать (f) *kravat'*
bee пчела (f) *pchila*
before до *do*, раньше *ran'she*
begin начинать/начать *nachinat'/nachat'*
beginner новичок (m) *navichok*
beginning начало (n) *nachala*; **at the beginning** в начале *v nachyali*
behind позади *pazadi*
Belarus Беларусь (f) *bilaroos*
Belgium Бельгия (f) *byel'giya*
believe верить/поверить *vyerit'/pavyerit'*
below внизу *vnizoo*, под *pat*
beside около *okala*
best лучший *lootshy*
better лучше *lootshe*; **to get better** улучшиться *oolootshytsa* поправиться *papravitsa*; **it's better to …** лучше было бы … *lootshe byla by …*
between между *myezhdoo*
bicycle велосипед (m) *vilasipyet*
bicycle pump насос (m) *nasos*
big большой *bal'shoi*
bike (*motorbike*) мотоцикл (m) *matatsykl*; (*bicycle*) велосипед (m) *vilasipyet*
bill счёт (m) *schyot* 51
bin мусорное ведро (n) *moosarnaye vidro*, урна (f) *oorna*
binoculars бинокль (m) *binokl'*
bird птица (f) *ptitsa*
birthday день рождения (m) *dyen' razhdyeniya*

bite (*noun*) укус (m) *ookoos*
bite (v) кусать/укусить *koosat'/ookoosit'* 104
black чёрный *chyorny*
blackout полное отключение (n) *polnaye atklyoochyeniye*
blanket одеяло (n) *adiyala*
bleed кровоточить *kravatochit'*
bless: bless you! будь здоров! *boot' zdarof!*
blind слепой *slipoi*
blister волдырь (m) *valdyr'*
blood кровь (f) *krof'*
blood pressure кровяное давление (n) *kravyanoye davlyeniye*
blue голубой *galooboi*; (*dark*) синий *sini*
board борт (m) *bort*
boarding посадка (f) *pasatka*
boat судно (n) *soodna*
body тело (n) *tyela*
book (*noun*) книга (f) *kniga*
book (v) бронировать/забронировать *braniravat'/zabraniravat'* 23
booking бронирование (n) *braniravaniye*
bookshop книжный магазин (m) *knizhny magazin*
boot ботинок (m) *batinok*; (*of car*) багажник (m) *bagazhnik*
borrow брать напрокат *brat' naprakat*
botanical garden ботанический сад (m) *batanichiski sat*
both оба *oba*; **both of us** мы вдвоём *my vdvayom*
bottle бутылка (f) *bootylka*
bottle opener штопор (m) *shtopar*
bottom дно (n) *dno*; **at the bottom** внизу *vnizoo*; **at the bottom of** на дне *na dnye*
bowl миска (f) *miska*, чаша (f) *chyasha*
bra бюстгальтер (m) *byoosgal'tir*
brake (*noun*) тормоз (m) *tormas*
brake (v) тормозить *tarmazit'*
bread хлеб (m) *Hlyep* 49

break ломать/сломать *lamat'/slamat'*; **to break one's leg** сломать ногу *slamat' nogoo*

break down сломаться *slamatsa* **32, 110**

breakdown поломка *(f) palomka*

breakdown service автосервис *(m) aftasyervis*

breakfast завтрак *(m) zaftrak* **39**; **to have breakfast** завтракать *zaftrakat'*

bridge мост *(m) most*

bring приносить/принести *prinasit'/prinis'ti*

brochure брошюра *(f) brashoora*

broken сломанный *slomany*

bronchitis бронхит *(m) branHit*

brother брат *(m) brat*

brown коричневый *karichnivy*

brush щётка *(f) schyotka*

build строить/построить *stroit'/pastroit'*

building здание *(n) zdaniye*

bump *(v)* стукнуться *stooknootsa*

bumper бампер *(m) bampir*

buoy буёк *(m) booyok*

burn *(noun)* ожог *(m) azhok*

burn гореть/сгореть *garyet'/zgaryet'*; **to burn oneself** обжигаться/обжечься *abzhygatsa/abzhechs'a*

burst *(v)* взрываться *vzryvatsa*

bus автобус *(m) aftoboos* **29**

bus route автобусный маршрут *(m) aftoboosny marshroot*

bus station автовокзал *(m) aftavagzal*

bus stop автобусная остановка *(f) aftoboosnaya astanofka*

busy занятый *zanyaty*

but но *no*

buy покупать/купить *pakoopat'/koopit'* **80, 83**

by на *na*; **by car** на машине *na mashyny*

bye! пока! *paka!*

C

café кафе *(n) kafe*

call *(v)* звать *zvat'*; *(on phone)* звонить *zvanit'* **99**

call back перезванивать/перезвонить *pirizvanivat'/pirizvanit'* **99, 100**

camera фотоаппарат *(m) fataaparat*

camping кемпинг *(m) kempink*

campsite кемпинг *(m) kempink* **42**

can *(v)* *(to be physically able)* мочь *moch (see grammar)*; *(to know how)* уметь *oomyet'*; **I can't** я не могу *ya ni magoo*

can *(noun)* банка *(f) banka*

cancel отменять/отменить *atminyat'/atminit'*

candle свеча *(f) svichya*

can opener открывалка *(f) atkryvalka*

car машина *(f) mashyna*

caravan фургон *(m) foorgon*

card карточка *(f) kartachka*

car park автостоянка *(f) aftastayanka*

carry носить/нести *nasit'/nis'ti*

case: in case of в случае *(+ gen.) f sloochii*

cash наличные *(pl) nalichnyyi*; **to pay cash** платить наличными *platit' nalichnymi* **37, 82**

cashpoint касса *(f) kasa* **91**

castle замок *(m) zamak*

catch ловить/поймать *lavit'/païmat'*

cathedral собор *(m) sabor*

CD CD диск *(m) CD disk*

cemetery кладбище *(n) kladbischye*

centimetre сантиметр *(m) santimyetr*

centre центр *(m) tsentr* **39**

century век *(m) vyek*

chair стул *(m) stool*

chairlift подъёмник *(m) pad-yomnik*

change *(noun)* изменение *(n) izminyeniye*; *(money)* сдача *(f) zdachya*, мелочь *(f) myelach'* **82**

change (v) менять/поменять minyat'/paminyat', разменивать/разменять razmyenivat'/razminyat' **29**, **91**

changing room примерочная primyerachnaya **84**

chapel часовня (f) chisovnya

charge (noun) цена (f) tsyna, стоимость (f) stoimast't

cheap дешёвый dishovy

check (v) проверять/проверить praviryat'/pravyerit'

check in регистрироваться/зарегистрироваться rigistriravatsa/zarigistriravatsa

check-in (at airport) регистрация (f) rigistratsyya **25**

check-out (at hotel) отъезд (m) at-yest; (in supermarket) касса (f) kasa

cheers! ура! oora!, Ваше здоровье! vashe zdarov'ye!

chemist's аптека (f) aptyeka

cheque чек (m) chyek

chest грудная клетка (f) groodnaya klyetka

child ребёнок (m) ribyonak

chimney труба (f) trooba, дымоход (m) dymaHot

chin подбородок (m) padbarodak

church церковь (f) tserkaf'

cigar сигара (f) sigara

cigarette сигарета (f) sigaryeta

cigarette paper сигаретная бумага (f) sigaryetnaya boomaga

cinema кино (n) kino

circus цирк (m) tsyrk

city город (m) gorat

clean (adj) чистый chisty

clean (v) убирать/убрать oobirat'/oobrat'

cliff крутой склон (m) krootoï sklon, скала (f) skala

climate климат (m) klimat

climbing скалолазание (n) skalalazaniye, альпинизм (m) al'pinizm

cloakroom гардероб (m) gardirop

close (v) закрывать/закрыть zakryvat'/zakryt'

closed закрытый zakryty

closing time время закрытия (n) vryemya zakrytiya

clothes одежда (f) adyezhda

clutch (noun) сцепление (n) stsyplyeniye

coach автобус (m) aftoboos **29**

coast берег (m) byerik, побережье (n) pabiryezh'ye

coathanger вешалка (f) vyeshalka

cockroach таракан (m) tarakan

coffee кофе (m) kofye

coil (contraceptive) спираль (f) spiral'

coin монета (f) manyeta

Coke® кола (f) kola

cold (adj) холодный Halodny; **it's cold** холодно Holadna; **I'm cold** мне холодно mnye Holadna

cold (noun) простуда (f) prastooda; **to have a cold** простудиться prastooditsa

collection коллекция (f) kalyektsyya

colour цвет (m) tsvyet **84**

comb расчёска (f) raschyoska

come приходить/прийти priHadit'/priïti

come back возвращаться/вернуться vazvrashchyatsa/virnootsa

come in входить/войти fHadit'/vaïti

come out выходить/выйти vyHadit'/vyïti

comfortable удобный oodobny, комфортабельный kamfartabil'ny

company компания (f) kampaniya

compartment (in train) купе (n) koope

complain жаловаться/пожаловаться zhalavatsa/pazhalavatsa

comprehensive insurance комплексная страховка (f) kompliksnaya straHofka

computer компьютер (m) kamp'yooter

concert концерт (m) kantsert **63**

concert hall концертный зал (m) kantsertny zal

concession льгота (f) l'gota **23**, **69**

condom презерватив (m) prizirvatif

confirm подтверждать/подтвердить *patvirzhdat'/patvirdit'* **25**

connection пересадка (f) *pirisatka*, связь (f) *svyas'* **26**

constipation запор (m) *zapor*

consulate консульство (n) *konsool'stva* **110**

contact (noun) контакт (m) *kantakt*

contact (v) связываться/связаться *svyazyvatsa/svizatsa*

contact lenses контактные линзы (fpl) *kantaktnyi linzy*

contagious заразный *zarazny*

contraceptive противозачаточное средство (n) *prativazachyatachnaye sryetstva*

cook (v) готовить/приготовить *gatovit'/prigatovit'*

cooked приготовленный *prigatovliny*, готовый *gatovy*

cooking готовка (f) *gatofka*; **to do the cooking** готовить *gatovit'*

cool прохладный *praHladny*

corkscrew штопор (m) *shtopar*

correct правильный *pravil'ny*

cost (v) стоить *stoit'*

cotton хлопок (m) *Hlopak*

cotton wool вата (f) *vata*

cough (noun) кашель (m) *kashyl'*; **to have a cough** кашлять *kashlit'*

cough (v) кашлять *kashlit'*

count (v) считать *schitat'*

country страна (f) *strana*

countryside сельская местность (f) *syel'skaya mesnas't'*

course: of course конечно *kanyeshna*

cover (noun) обложка (f) *abloshka*, крышка (f) *kryshka*

cover (v) накрывать/накрыть *nakryvat'/nakryt'*

credit card кредитная карта (f) *kriditnaya karta* **37, 51, 82**

cross (noun) крест (m) *kryest*

cross (v) переходить/перейти *piriHadit'/piriïti*

cruise круиз (m) *kroois*

cry плакать/заплакать *plakat'/zaplakat'*

cup чашка (f) *chyashka*

currency валюта (f) *valyoota*

customs таможня (f) *tamozhnya*

cut (v) резать *ryezat'*; **to cut oneself** обрезаться *abryezatsa*

cycle path велосипедная дорожка (f) *vilasipyednaya daroshka* **77**

D

damaged повреждённый *pavrizhdyony*

damp влажный *vlazhny*

dance (noun) танец (m) *tanits*

dance (v) танцевать *tantsyvat'*

dangerous опасный *apasny*

dark тёмный *tyomny*; **dark blue** синий *sini*

date (noun) число (n) *chislo*; **out of date** устаревший *oostaryefshi*, несовременный *nisavrimyeny*

date of birth дата рождения (f) *data razhdyeniya*

daughter дочь (f) *doch*

day день (m) *dyen'*; **the day after tomorrow** послезавтра *poslizaftra*; **the day before yesterday** позавчера *pozafchira*

dead мёртвый *myortvy*

deaf глухой *glooHoï*

dear дорогой *daragoï*

debit card дебетовая карта (f) *debitovaya karta*

December декабрь (m) *dikabr'*

declare декларировать/ задекларировать *diklariravat'/ zadiklariravat'*

deep глубокий *glooboki*

degree степень (f) *styepin'*, градус (m) *gradoos*

delay задержка (f) *zadyershka*

delayed задержанный *zadyerzhany*

deli деликатес (m) *dilikates*, кулинария (f) *koolinariya*

dentist стоматолог (m) *stamatolak*

deodorant дезодорант *(m) dizadarant*

department отдел *(m) adyel*

department store универмаг *(m) ooniirmak*

departure отъезд *(m) at-yest*

depend: that depends (on) это зависит от (+ gen.) *eta zavisit at*

deposit залог *(m) zalok*

dessert десерт *(m) disyert* **48**

develop: to get a film developed проявлять/проявить плёнку *prayavlyat'/prayavit' plyonkoo* **88**

diabetes диабет *(m) diabet*

dialling code телефонный код *(m) tilifony kot*

diarrhoea: to have diarrhoea у меня расстройство желудка *oo minya rastroïstva zhylootka*

die умереть *oomiryet'*

diesel дизельный *dizil'ny*

diet диета *(f) diyeta;* **to be on a diet** сидеть на диете *sidyet' na diyeti*

different разный *razny;* **different from** отличный от (+ gen.) *atlichny at*

difficult сложный *slozhny*

digital camera цифровой фотоаппарат *(m) tsyfravoï fataaparat*

dinner ужин *(m) oozhyn;* **to have dinner** ужинать *oozhynat'*

direct прямой *primoï*

direction направление *(n) napravlyeniye;* **to have a good sense of direction** хорошо ориентироваться *Harasho arintiravatsa*

directory справочник *(m) spravachnik*

directory enquiries справочная *(f) spravachnaya*

dirty грязный *gryazny*

disabled неспособный *nispasobny* **111;** **disabled person** инвалид *(m) invalit*

disaster стихийное бедствие *(n) stiHiïnaye byetsviye*

disco дискотека *(f) diskatyeka*

discount скидка *(f) skitka* **69;** **to give a discount** сделать скидку *z'dyelat' skitkoo*

discount fare льготный тариф *(m) l'gotny tarif*

dish блюдо *(n) blyooda;* **dish of the day** блюдо дня *(n) blyooda dnya*

dishes посуда *(f) pasooda;* **to do the dishes** мыть посуду *myt' pasoodoo*

dish towel кухонное полотенце *(n) kooHonaye palatyentse*

dishwasher посудомоечная машина *(f) pasoodamoïchnaya mashyna*

disinfect дезинфицировать *dizinfitsyryvat'*

disposable одноразовый *adnarazavy*

disturb беспокоить *bispakoit';* **do not disturb** просьба не беспокоить *proz'ba ni bispakoit'*

dive нырять *nyryat'*

diving: to go diving заниматься подводным плаванием *zanimatsa padvodnym plavan'yem*

do делать/сделать *dyelat'/z'dyelat'*

doctor врач *(m) vrach* **103, 110**

door дверь *(f) dvyer'*

door code код *(m) kot*

downstairs вниз по лестнице *vnis pa lyesnitsy*

draught beer разливное пиво *(n) razlivnoye piva*

dress: to get dressed одеться *adyetsa*

dressing приправа *(f) priprava*

drink (noun) напиток *(m) napitak;* **to go for a drink** пойти выпить *païti vypit'* **45, 60;** **to have a drink** выпить *vypit'*

drink (v) пить/выпить *pit'/vypit'*

drinking water питьевая вода *(f) pit'ivaya vada*

drive (noun) **to go for a drive** покататься на машине *pakatatsa na mashyni*

drive (v) вести машину *vis'ti mashynoo*

driving licence водительские права *(pl) vaditil'skii prava*

drops капли *(pl) kapli*

drown тонуть *tanoot'*

drugs (medication) лекарства (pl) likarstva; (narcotics) наркотики (pl) narkotiki

drunk пьяный p'yany

dry (adj) сухой sooHoï

dry (v) сушить/высушить sooshyt'/ vysooshyt'

dry cleaner's химчистка (f) Himchistka

duck утка (f) ootka

during в течение f tichyenii; **during the week** в течение недели f tichyenii nidyeli

dustbin мусорная корзина (f) moosarnaya karzina

duty chemist's дежурная аптека (f) dizhoornaya aptyeka

E

each каждый kazhdy; **each one** каждый kazhdy

ear ухо (n) ooHa

early рано rana

earplugs ушные тампоны (pl) ooshnyi tampony

earrings серёжки (pl) siryoshki

earth земля (f) zimlya

east восток (m) vastok; **in the east** на востоке na vastoki; **(to the) east of** к востоку от k vastokoo at

Easter Пасха (f) pasHa

easy легко liHko

eat есть yes't' **45**

economy class эконом класс (m) ekanom klas

Elastoplast® лейкопластырь (m) liikaplastyr'

electric электрический iliktrichiski

electric shaver электробритва (f) iliktrabritva

electricity электричество (n) iliktrichistva

electricity meter счётчик (m) schyochik

e-mail электронная почта (f) iliktronaya pochta

e-mail address электронный адрес (m) iliktrony adris **17, 95**

embassy посольство (n) pasol'stva **110**

emergency срочность (f) srochnas't'; **in an emergency** в срочном порядке f srochnam paryatki

emergency exit аварийный выход (m) avariiny vyHat

empty пустой poostoï

end конец (m) kanyets; **at the end of** в конце (+ gen.) f kantse; **at the end of the street** в конце улицы f kantse oolitsy

engaged помолвлен pamolvlin

engine двигатель (m) dvigatil'

England Англия (f) angliya

English (adj) английский angliski

Englishman англичанин (m) anglichyanin

Englishwoman англичанка (f) anglichyanka

enjoy: enjoy your meal! приятного аппетита! priyatnava apitita!; **to enjoy oneself** хорошо проводить/ провести время Harasho pravadit'/ pravis'ti vryemya

enough достаточно dastatachna; **that's enough** этого хватит etava Hvatit

entrance вход (m) fHot

envelope конверт (m) kanvyert

epileptic эпилептический epiliptichiski

equipment оборудование (n) abaroodavaniye

espresso эспрессо (n) espresa

Europe Европа (f) Yevropa

European (adj) европейский yevrapeïski

evening вечер (m) vyechir; **in the evening** вечером vyechiram

every каждый kazhdy; **every day** каждый день kazhdy dyen'

everybody, everyone каждый kazhdy (sg), все fsye (pl)

everywhere всюду fsyoodoo, везде viz'dye

except за исключением *za isklyoochyeniim*

exceptional исключительный *isklyoochitil'ny*

excess излишек *(m) izlishek*, избыток *(m) izbytak*

exchange обмен *(m) abmyen*

exchange rate курс обмена *(m) koors abmyena*

excuse *(noun)* извинение *(n) izvinyeniye*

excuse *(v)* excuse me извините меня *izviniti minya*

exhaust исчерпывать *ischyerpyvat'*, утомлять *ootamlyat'*

exhausted утомлённый *ootamlyony*

exhaust pipe выхлопная труба *(f) vyHlapnaya trooba*

exhibition выставка *(f) vystafka* **68**

exit выход *(m) vyHat*

expensive дорогой *daragoï*

expiry date срок годности *(m) srok godnas'ti*, срок действия *(m) srok dyeïstviya*

explosion взрыв *(m) vzryf*

express *(m)* экспресс *ikspryes*

extra дополнительно *dapalnitil'na*

eye глаз *(m) glas*

F

face лицо *(n) litso*

facecloth мочалка *(f) machyalka*

fact факт *(m) fakt*; **in fact** на самом деле *na samam dyeli*

faint *(v)* упасть в обморок *obmarak*

fair *(noun)* ярмарка *(f) yarmarka*

fall падать/упасть *padat'/oopas't'*; **to fall asleep** засыпать/заснуть *zasypat'/zasnoot'*; **to fall ill** заболевать/заболеть *zabalivat'/zabalyet'*

family семья *(f) sim'ya*

far далеко *daliko*; **far from** далеко от *(+ gen.) daliko at*

fare плата *(f) plata*, тариф *(m) tarif*

fast быстрый *bystry*

fast-food restaurant ресторан быстрого обслуживания *(m) ristaran bystrava apsloozhyvaniya*

fat жирный *zhyrny*

father отец *(m) atyets*

favour *(f)* услуга *ooslooga*; **to do someone a favour** оказать кому-нибудь услугу *akazat' kamoo-niboot' oosloogoo*

favourite любимый *lyoobimy*

fax факс *(m) faks*

February февраль *(m) fivral'*

fed up надоесть *nadayes't'*; **I'm fed up with …** мне … *(+ nom.)* надоело *mnye … nadayela*

feel чувствовать *chyoostvavat'*; **to feel good/bad** хорошо/плохо себя чувствовать *Harasho/ploHa sibya chyoostvavat'*

feeling чувство *(n) chyoostva*

ferry паром *(m) parom*

festival фестиваль *(m) fistival'*

fetch: to go and fetch someone позвать кого-нибудь *pazvat' kavo-niboot'*; **to go and fetch something** принести что-нибудь *prinisti shto-niboot'*

fever температура *(f) timpiratoora*; **I have a fever** у меня температура *oo minya timpiratoora*

few мало *mala*

fiancé жених *(m) zhyniH*

fiancée невеста *(f) nivyesta*

fight драка *(f) draka*

fill наполнять/наполнить *napalnyat'/napolnit'*

fill in заполнять/заполнить *zapalnyat'/zapolnit'*

fill up: to fill up with petrol заправлять/заправить бензином *zapravlyat'/zapravit'*

filling *(in tooth)* пломба *(f) plomba*

film *(for camera)* плёнка *(f) plyonka*; *(movie)* фильм *(m) fil'm* **62, 88**

finally в конце концов *f kantse kantsov*

find находить/найти *naHadit'/naiti*

fine (adj) нормальный *narmal'ny*; **I'm fine** я в порядке *ya f paryatki*

fine (noun) штраф (m) *shtraf*

finger палец (m) *palits*

finish заканчивать/закончить *zakanchivat'/zakonchit'*

fire огонь (m) *agon'*; **fire!** пожар! *pazhar!*

fire brigade пожарные (pl) *pazharnyi*

fireworks фейерверк (m) *fiyerverk*

first первый *pyervy*; **first (of all)** прежде всего *prezhdi fsivo*

first class первый класс (m) *pyervy klas*

first floor второй этаж (m) *ftaroi etash*

first name имя (n) *imya*

fish (noun) рыба (f) *ryba*

fish counter рыбный отдел (m) *rybny adyel*

fishmonger's, fish shop рыбный магазин (m) *rybny magazin*

fitting room примерочная (f) *primyerachnaya*

fizzy газированный *gazirovany*

flash вспышка (f) *fspyshka*

flask термос (m) *termas*, фляга (f) *flyaga*

flat (adj) плоский *ploski*; **flat tyre** спущенная шина (f) *spooschinaya shyna*

flat (noun) квартира (f) *kvartira*

flavour вкус (m) *fkoos*

flight рейс (m) *ryeïs*

flip-flops шлёпки (pl) *shlyopki*

floor пол (m) *pol*; **on the floor** на полу *na paloo*

flu грипп (m) *grip*

fly (noun) муха (f) *mooHa*

fly (v) летать *litat'*

food еда (f) *yida*

food poisoning пищевое отравление (n) *pischivoye atravlyeniye*

foot нога (f) *naga*, ступня (f) *stoopnya*

for для *dlya*; **for an hour** на час *na chyas*, в течение часа *v tichyenii chyasa*

forbidden запрещённый *zaprischony*

forecast прогноз (m) *prognos*

forehead лоб (m) *lop*

foreign иностранный *inastrany*

foreigner иностранец (m) *inastranits*, иностранка (f) *inastranka*

forest лес (m) *lyes*

fork вилка (f) *vilka*

former бывший *byfshy*

forward (adj) передний *piryedni*

forwards вперёд *vpiryot*

fracture перелом (m) *pirilom*

fragile хрупкий *Hroopki*

France Франция (f) *frantsyya*

free бесплатный *bisplatny* 67

freezer морозилка (f) *marazilka*

Friday пятница (f) *pyatnitsa*

fridge холодильник (m) *Haladil'nik*

fried жареный *zhariny*

friend друг (m) *drook*, подруга (f) *padrooga*

from от *at*, из *iz*; **from ... to ...** от ... до ... *at ... do ...*

front: in front of впереди (+ gen.) *vpiridi*

front (adj) передний *piryedni*

fry (v) жарить *zharit'*

frying pan сковородка (f) *skavarotka*

full полный *polny*; **full of** полный (+ instr.) *polny*

full board полный пансион (m) *polny pansion*

full fare, full price полный тариф (m) *polny tarif*, полная стоимость (f) *polnaya stoimos't'* 69

funfair парк аттракционов (m) *park atraktsyonaf*

fuse пробка (f) *propka*

G

gallery галерея (f) *galiryeya*

game игра (f) igra **77**, **78**
garage гараж (m) garash **32**
garden сад (m) sat
gas газ (m) gas
gas cylinder газовый баллон (m) gazavy balon
gastric flu желудочный грипп (m) zhyloodachny grip
gate ворота (f) varota
gauze марля (f) marlya
gay (adj) гомосексуальный (m) gamasyksooal'ny, лесбийская (f) lizbiïskaya
gearbox коробка передач (f) karopka piridach
general общий opschi
gents' (toilet) мужской туалет (m) moozhskoï tooalyet
German (adj) немецкий nimyetski
German (noun) немец (m) nyemits, немка (f) nyemka
Germany Германия (f) Girmaniya
get получать/получить paloochyat'/ paloochit'
get off сходить/сойти sHadit'/saïti **29**
get up вставать/встать fstavat'/fstat'; подниматься/подняться padnimatsa/ padnyatsa
gift wrap подарочная упаковка (f) padarachnaya oopakofka
girl девушка (f) dyevooshka
girlfriend девушка (f) dyevooshka
give давать/дать davat'/dat'
give back возвращать/вернуть vazvrashchyat'/virnoot'
glass стакан (m) stakan; **a glass of water/wine** стакан воды/вина stakan vady/vina
glasses очки (pl) achki
go идти iti, ехать yeHat'; **to go to London/the UK** ехать в Лондон/ Великобританию yeHat' v London/ Vilikabritaniyoo; **we're going home tomorrow** завтра мы едем домой zaftra my yedem damoï

go away уезжать/уехать ooizhat'/ ooyeHat'
go in входить/войти fHadit'/vaïti
go out выходить/выйти vyHadit'/vyïti
go with сопровождать/сопроводить sapravazhdat'/sapravadit'
golf гольф (m) gol'f
good хороший Haroshy; **good morning** доброе утро dobraye ootra; **good afternoon** добрый день dobry dyen'; **good evening** добрый вечер dobry vyechir
goodbye до свидания da svidaniya
goodnight спокойной ночи spakoïnaï nochi
goods товары (mpl) tavary
GP терапевт (m) tirapyeft
grams граммы (pl) gramy **83**
grass трава (f) trava
great великий viliki
Great Britain Великобритания (f) vilikabritaniya
Greece Греция (f) gryetsyya
green зелёный zilyony
grey серый syery
grocer's бакалея (f) bakalyeya
ground земля (f) zimlya; **on the ground** на земле na zimlye
ground floor первый этаж (m) pyervy etash
grow расти/вырасти ras'ti/vyras'ti
guarantee гарантировать garantiravat'
guest гость (m) gos't
guest house домик для гостей (m) domik dlya gas'tyeï
guide экскурсовод (m) ikskoorsavot **62**, **67**
guidebook путеводитель (m) pootivaditil'
guided tour экскурсия (f) ikskoorsiya
gynaecologist гинеколог (m) ginikolak

H

hair волосы (mpl) volasy

hairdresser парикмахер *(m) parikmaHir*

hairdryer фен *(m) fyen*

half половина *(f) palavina;* **half a litre** пол-литра *pol-litra;* **half a kilo** полкило *polkilo;* **half an hour** полчаса *polchisa*

half-board полупансион *(m) poloopansion*

hand рука *(f) rooka*

handbag дамская сумочка *(f) damskaya soomachka*

handbrake ручной тормоз *(m) roochnoï tormas*

handkerchief носовой платок *(m) nasavoï platok*

hand luggage ручная кладь *(f) roochnaya klat'* 25

hangover похмелье *(n) paHmyel'ye*

happen случаться/случиться *sloochyatsa/sloochitsa*

happy счастливый *schislivy*

hard *(difficult)* трудный *troodny;* *(solid)* жёсткий *zhostki*

hat шапка *(f) shapka*

hate ненавидеть *ninavidit'*

have иметь *imyet'*

have to должен/должна *dolzhyn/dalzhna;* **I have to go** мне нужно идти *mnye noozhna iti*

hay fever сенная лихорадка *(f) sinaya liHaratka*

he он *on*

head голова *(f) galava*

headache: I have a headache у меня болит голова *oo minya balit galava*

headlight передняя фара *(f) piryednyaya fara*

health здоровье *(n) zdarov'ye*

hear слышать/услышать *slyshat'/ooslyshat'*

heart сердце *(n) syertse*

heart attack сердечный приступ *(m) sirdyechny pristoop*

heat жара *(f) zhara*

heating отопление *(n) ataplyeniye*

heavy тяжёлый *tizholy*

hello здравствуйте *zdrastvooïti*

helmet каска *(f) kaska*

help *(noun)* помощь *(f) pomasch;* **to call for help** звать на помощь *zvat' na pomasch;* **help!** помогите! *pamagiti!*

help *(v)* помогать/помочь *pamagat'/pamoch* 109

her её *yiyo*

here здесь *z'dyes';* **here is/are** вот *vot*

hers её *yiyo*

hi! привет! *privyet!*

hi-fi hi-fi *haï-faï*

high высокий *vysoki*

high blood pressure высокое давление *(n) vysokaye davlyeniye*

high tide прилив *(m) prilif*

hiking: to go hiking ходить в походы *Hadit' v paHody* 75

hill холм *(m) Holm,* гора *(f) gara*

him его *yivo,* ему *yimoo,* им *im*

himself сам *sam*

hip бедро *(n) bidro*

hire *(noun)* наём *(m) naïm,* прокат *(m) prakat* 33, 73, 76, 77

hire *(v)* снимать *snimat',* брать в прокат *brat' v prakat*

his его *yivo*

hitchhiking автостоп *(m) aftastop,* путешествие автостопом *(n) pootishestviye aftastopom*

hold держать *dirzhat'*

hold on! *(on the phone)* оставаться на линии! *astavatsa na linii!*

holiday отпуск *otpoosk,* каникулы *kanikooly;* **I'm on holiday** я в отпуске *ya v otpooski*

holiday camp дом отдыха *(m) dom otdyHa*

Holland Голландия *(f) Galandiya*

home дом *(m) dom;* **at home** дома *doma;* **to go home** возвращаться домой *vazvraschyatsa damoï*

honest честный *chyesny*

honeymoon медовый месяц *(m) midovy myesits*

horse лошадь *(f) loshit'*

hospital больница *(f) bal'nitsa*

hot жаркий *zharki;* **it's hot** жарко *zharka;* **hot chocolate** горячий шоколад *(m) garyachi shykalat;* **hot drink** горячий напиток *(m) garyachi napitak*

hotel гостиница *(f) gastinitsa*

hour час *(m) chyas;* **an hour and a half** полтора часа *paltara chisa*

house дом *(m) dom*

housework работа по дому *(f) rabota pa domoo;* **to do the housework** заниматься хозяйством *zanimatsa Hazyaïstvam*

how как *kak;* **how are you?** как дела? *kak dila?*

hunger голод *(m) golat*

hungry: to be hungry проголодаться *pragaladatsa*

hurry: hurry up! поторапливайтесь! *pataraplivaïts'!*

hurry: to be in a hurry торопиться *taropitsa*

hurt: it hurts болеть *balyet'* 105; **my head hurts** у меня болит голова *oo minya balit galava*

husband муж *(m) moosh*

I

I я *ya;* **I'm English** я англичанин/ англичанка *ya anglichyanin/ anglichyanka;* **I'm 22 (years old)** мне двадцать два года *mne dvatsat' dva goda*

ice лёд *(m) lyot*

ice cube кубик льда *(m) koobik l'da*

identity card удостоверение личности *(n) oodastviryeniye lichnasti*

identity papers документы *(pl) dakoomyenty*

if если *yesli*

ill больной *bal'noï*

illness болезнь *(f) balyez'n'*

important важный *vazhny*

in в *v;* **in England** в Англии *v anglii;* **in 2007** в 2007 году *v 2007 gadoo;* **in the 19th century** в девятнадцатом веке *v divitnatsatom vyeki;* **in an hour** через час *chiris chyas*

included включён *fklyoochyon* 39, 41, 51

independent независимый *nizavisimy*

indicator указатель *(m) ookazatil'*

infection инфекция *(f) infektsyya*

information информация *(f) infarmatsyya* 67

injection укол *(m) ookol*

injured травмированный *travmiravany*

insect насекомое *(n) nasikomaye*

insecticide средство от насекомых *(n) sretstva at nasikomyH*

inside внутрь *vnootr',* внутри *vnootri*

insomnia бессонница *(f) bisonitsa*

instant coffee быстрорастворимый кофе *(m) bystrarastvarimy kofi*

instead вместо *vmyesta;* **instead of** вместо *(+ gen.) vmyesta*

insurance страховка *(f) straHofka*

intend: to intend to намереваться сделать что-либо *namirivatsa z'dyelat' shto-liba*

international международный *myizhdoonarodny*

international money order международный денежный перевод *(m) mizhdoonarodny dyenizhny pirivot*

Internet Интернет *(m) intyrnet*

Internet café Интернет кафе *(n) intyrnet kafe* 95

invite приглашать/пригласить *priglashat'/priglasit'*

Ireland Ирландия *(f) irlandiya*

Irish ирландский *irlanski*

Irishman ирландец *(m) irlandits*

Irishwoman ирландка *(f) irlantka*

iron (noun) утюг *(m) ootyook*

iron (v) гладить/погладить *gladit'/pagladit'*

island остров *(m) ostraf*

it это *eta*; оно *ano*; **it's beautiful** это красиво *eta krasiva*; **it's warm** тепло *tiplo*

Italian (adj) итальянский *ital'yanski*

Italian (noun) итальянец (m) *ital'yanits*, итальянка (f) *ital'yanka*

Italy Италия (f) *italiya*

itchy: it's itchy чешется *chyeshytsa*

item единица (f) *yidinitsa*, пункт (m) *poonkt*

jacket куртка (f) *koortka*

January январь (m) *yinvar'*

jetlag акклиматизация (f) *aklimatizatsyya*

jeweller's ювелирный магазин (m) *yoovilirny magazin*

jewellery ювелирные изделия (pl) *yoovilyirnyyi izdyeliya*

job работа (f) *rabota*

jogging бег трусцой (m) *byek troostsoï*

journey путешествие (n) *pootishestviye*

jug кувшин (m) *koofshyn*

juice сок (m) *sok*

July июль (m) *iyool'*

jumper свитер (m) *svityr*

June июнь (m) *iyoon'*

just: just a little немного *nimnoga*; **just one** только один *tol'ka adin*; **I've just arrived** я только приехал (m)/приехала (f) *ya tol'ka priyeHal/priyeHala*; **just in case** на всякий случай *na fsyaki sloochii*

kayak байдарка (f) *baïdarka*

keep хранить/сохранить *Hranit'/saHranit'*

key ключ (m) *klyooch* **40**, **41**

kidney почка (f) *pochka*

kill убивать/убить *oobivat'/oobit'*

kilogram килограмм *kilagram* **83**

kilometre километр (m) *kilamyetr*

kind: what kind of …? какой …? *kakoï …?*

kitchen кухня (f) *kooHnya*

knee колено (n) *kalyena*

knife нож (m) *nosh*

knock down сбить *zbit'*, опрокинуть *aprakinut'*

know знать *znat'*; **I don't know** я не знаю *ya ni znayoo*

ladies' (toilet) женский туалет (m) *zhenski tooalyet*

lake озеро (n) *ozira*

lamp лампа (f) *lampa*

land (plane) приземляться/приземлиться *prizimlyatsa/prizimlitsa*

landscape пейзаж (m) *piïzash*

language язык (m) *yizyk*

laptop ноутбук (m) *no-ootbook*

last (adj) последний *paslyedni*; **last year** в прошлом году f *proshlam gadoo*

last (v) длиться *dlitsa*

late поздний *pozni*

latte латтэ (m) *late*

laugh смеяться *smiyatsa*

launderette прачечная (f) *prachichnaya*

lawyer адвокат (m) *advakat*

leaflet листовка (f) *listofka*, проспект (m) *praspyekt*

leak (v) течь *tyech'*, протекать *pratikat'*

learn учить/выучить *oochit'/vyoochit'*, узнать *ooznat'*

least: the least минимальный *minimal'ny*; **at least** по крайней мере *pa kraïnii myeri*

leave уходить *ooHadit'*, оставлять *astavlyat'*

left левый *lyevy*; **to the left (of)** налево от (+ gen.) *nalyeva at*

left-luggage (office) камера хранения (f) *kamira Hranyeniya*

leg нога (f) *naga*

lend одолжать *adalzhyt'*

lens (of camera) объектив (m) ab-iktif
lenses линзы (pl) linzy
less меньше men'she; **less than**
менее, чем myeniye, chyem
let пускать pooskat'; разрешать
razrishat'
letter письмо (n) pis'mo
letterbox почтовый ящик (m)
pachtovy yashik
library библиотека (f) bibliatyeka
life жизнь (f) zhyz'n'
lift лифт (m) lift **39**
light (adj) лёгкий lyoHki; **light blue**
светло-голубой svetla-galoobo'i
light (noun) свет (m) svyet; **do
you have a light?** прикурить не
найдётся? prikoorit' ni naïdyotsa?
light (v) зажигать/зажечь zazhygat'/
zazhech
light bulb прозрачная лампочка (f)
prazrachnaya lampachka
lighter зажигалка (f) zazhygalka
lighthouse маяк (m) mayak
like (adv) похожий paHozhy
like (v) любить lyoobit'; **I'd like … я
бы хотел (m)/хотела (f) ya by Hatyel/
Hatyela **18**
line линия (f) liniya **29**
lip губа (f) gooba
listen слушать slooshat'
litre литр (m) litr **32**
little (adj) маленький malin'ki
little (adv) мало mala
live жить zhyt'
liver печень (f) pyechin'
living room гостиная (f) gastinaya
local time местное время (n)
myesnaye vryemya
lock (v) запирать/запереть zapirat'/
zapiryet'
long длинный dliny; **a long time**
долгое время dolgaye vryemya; **how
long … ?** сколько …? skol'ko …?
look выглядеть vyglyadet'; **to look
tired** выглядеть усталым vyglyadet'
oostalym

look after присматривать/
присмотреть prismatrivat'/prismatryet'
look at смотреть на smatryet' na
look for искать iskat' **80**
look like быть похожим byt'
puHozhym
lorry грузовик (m) groozavik
lose терять/потерять tiryat'/patiryat'
32, 110; to get lost потеряться
patiryatsa; **I'm lost** я заблудился
(m)/ заблудилась (f) ya zabloodilsya/
zabloodilas' **12**
lot: a lot (of) много mnoga
loud громкий gromki
low низкий niski
low blood pressure низкое
давление (n) niskaye davlyeniye
low-calorie низкокалорийный
niskakalariïny
low tide отлив (m) atlif
luck удача (f) oodachya
lucky: I was lucky мне повезло mnye
pavizlo
luggage багаж (m) bagash **25**
lukewarm тёплый tyoply
lunch обед (m) abyet; **to have lunch**
обедать abyedat'
lung лёгкое (n) lyoHkaye
luxurious роскошный raskoshny
luxury роскошь (f) roskash

M

magazine журнал (m) zhoornal
maiden name девичья фамилия (f)
dyevich'ya familiya
mail почта (f) pochta
main главный glavny
main course главное блюдо (n)
glavnaye blyooda
make делать dyelat'
man человек (m) chilavyek
manage справляться spravlyatsa; **to
manage to do something** суметь
сделать что-либо soomyet' z'dyelat'
shto-liba

manager менеджер *(m)* m*e*nedzher
many много *mn*o*g*a; **how many?** сколько? skol'ka?; **how many times …?** сколько раз …? skol'ka ras …?
map карта *(f)* k*a*rta **12, 28, 61, 67**
March март *(m)* mart
market рынок *(m)* r*y*nak **83**
married *(man)* женатый zhyn*a*ty; *(woman)* замужем zam*oo*zhym
mass масса *(f)* m*a*ssa
match *(for fire)* спичка *(f)* sp*i*chka; *(game)* матч *(m)* mach
material материал *(m)* matir'y*a*l
matter: it doesn't matter это неважно *e*ta niv*a*zhna
mattress матрас *(m)* matr*a*s
May май *(m)* mai
maybe может быть m*o*zhyt byt'
me мне mnye, меня min*ya*, мной mnoi (see grammar); **me too** я тоже ya t*o*zhy
mean значить zn*a*chit'; **what does … mean?** что значит …? shto zn*a*chit …?
medicine лекарство *(n)* lik*a*rstva
medium средний sr*ye*dni
meet *(someone)* встречать fstrich*ya*t'; *(two people)* встречаться fstrich*ya*tsa **61**
meeting встреча *(f)* fstr*ye*chya, собрание *(n)* sabr*a*niye
member член *(m)* chlyen
menu меню *(n)* min*yo*o **47**
message сообщение *(n)* saapsch*ye*niye **98**
meter счётчик *(m)* sch*yo*chik
metre метр *(m)* myetr
microwave микроволновая печь *(f)* mikrav*a*ln*o*vaya pyech
midday полдень *(m)* p*o*ldin'
middle середина *(f)* sirid*i*na; **in the middle (of)** в середине (+ gen.) f sirid*i*ni
midnight полночь *(f)* p*o*lnach
might: it might rain возможно, будет дождь vazm*o*zhna, b*oo*dit dosht'

mill мельница *(f)* my*e*l'nitsa
mind: I don't mind я не против ya ni pr*o*tif
mine мой m*o*i, моя m*a*ya, моё m*o*yo (see grammar)
mineral water минеральная вода *(f)* mini*a*l'naya vad*a*
minute минута *(f)* min*oo*ta; **at the last minute** в последний момент f pasl*ye*dni mam*ye*nt
mirror зеркало *(n)* z*ye*rkala
Miss мисс mis
miss пропустить prapoos't*i*t' **30**; **we missed the train** мы опоздали на поезд my apazd*a*li na p*o*ist; **there are two … missing** не хватает двух … ni Hvat*a*it dvooH …
mistake ошибка *(f)* ash*y*pka **51**; **to make a mistake** допустить ошибку dapoos't*i*t' ash*y*pkoo
mobile (phone) мобильный телефон *(m)* mab*i*l'ny tilif*o*n **98**
modern современный savr*i*m*ye*ny
moisturizer увлажнитель *(m)* oovlazhn*i*til'
moment момент *(m)* mam*ye*nt; **at the moment** в настоящее время v nast*a*ya*schiye vr*ye*mya; **wait a moment** минуточку min*oo*tachkoo
monastery монастырь *(m)* manast*y*r'
Monday понедельник *(m)* panid*ye*l'nik
money деньги *(pl)* d*ye*n'gi
month месяц *(m)* m*ye*sits
monument памятник *(m)* p*a*mitnik
mood: to be in a good/bad mood быть в хорошем/плохом настроении byt' v Har*o*shym/plaH*o*m nastray*e*nii
moon луна *(f)* loon*a*
moped мопед *(m)* map*ye*t
more больше b*o*l'she; **more than** больше, чем b*o*l'she, chyem; **much more, a lot more** гораздо больше gar*a*zda b*o*l'she; **there's no more …** больше нет … b*o*l'she nyet …
morning утро *(n)* *oo*tra

Moscow Москва *(f) maskva*
mosque мечеть *(f) michyet'*
mosquito комар *(m) kamar*
most: the most большинство *(n)*
bal'shynstvo; **most people** большинство
людей *bal'shynstvo lyoodyeї*
mother мама *(f) mama*
motorbike мотоцикл *(m) matatsykl*
motorway автострада *(f) aftastrada*
mountain гора *(f) gara*
mountain bike горный велосипед
(m) gorny vilasipyet
mountain hut горная хижина *(f)*
gornaya Hizhyna
mouse мышь *(f) mysh*
mouth рот *(m) rot*
movie фильм *(m) fil'm*
Mr господин *gaspadin*
Mrs госпожа *gaspazha*
much: how much? сколько? *skol'ka?;*
**how much is it?, how much does
it cost?** сколько это стоит? *skol'ka
eta stoit?* **81**
muscle мышца *(f) myshtsa*
museum музей *(m) moozyeї*
music музыка *(f) moozyka*
must должен/должна *dolzhyn/dalzhna;*
it must be 5 o'clock сейчас,
должно быть, пять часов *sichyas,
dalzhno byt', pyat' chisof;* **I must go** я
должен идти *ya dolzhyn iti*
my мой *moї,* моя *maya,* моё *mayo,*
мои *maї (see grammar)*
myself себя *sibya*

N

nail *(on finger or toe)* ноготь *(m) nogat'*
naked раздетый *razdyety*
name имя *(n) imya* **37, 46; my name
is ...** меня зовут ... *minya zavoot ...*
14
nap дремота *(f) drimota;* **to have a
nap** вздремнуть *vzdrimnoot'*
napkin салфетка *(f) salfyetka*
nappy подгузник *(m) padgooz'nik*

national holiday национальный
праздник *(m) natsy-anal'ny praz'nik*
nature природа *(f) priroda*
near около *okala;* **near the beach**
около пляжа *okala plyazha;* **the
nearest** ближайший *blizhaїshy*
necessary нужный *noozhny,*
необходимый *niapHadimy*
neck шея *(f) sheya*
need нуждаться *noozhdatsa* **80**
neighbour сосед *(m) sasyet*
neither: neither do I я тоже не *ya
tozhe ni;* **neither ... nor ...** ни ...ни
... *ni ... ni ...*
nervous нервный *nyervny*
Netherlands Нидерланды *(pl)*
nidirlandy
never никогда *nikagda*
new новый *novy*
New Year Новый Год *(m) novy got*
news новость *(f) novas't'*
newsagent продавец газет *(m)
pradavyets gazyet*
newspaper газета *(f) gazyeta*
newspaper kiosk газетный киоск *(m)
gazyetny kiosk*
next следующий *slyedooschi*
nice милый *mily*
night ночь *(f) noch* **39, 42, 43**
nightclub ночной клуб *(m) nachnoї
kloop*
nightdress ночная рубашка *(f)
nachnaya roobashka*
no нет *nyet;* **no, thank you** нет,
спасибо *nyet, spasiba;* **no idea** не
знаю *ni znayoo*
nobody никто *nikto*
noise шум *(m) shoom;* **to make a
noise** шуметь *shoomyet'*
noisy шумный *shoomny*
non-drinking water вода из-под
крана *(f) vada is-pat krana*
none ни один *(m) ni adin,* ни одна *(f)
ni adna,* ни одно *(n) ni adno*
non-smoker некурящий *(m)
nikooryaschi,* некурящая *(f) nikooryaschiya*

noon полдень *(m) poldin'*

north север *(m) syevir;* **in the north** на севере *na syeviri;* **(to the) north of** на севере от *(+ gen.) na syeviri at*

nose нос *(m) nos*

not не *ni;* **not yet** ещё нет *ischyo;* **not any** ни одного *(m)*/ни одной *(f) ni adnavo/ni adnoï;* **not at all** совсем нет *safsyem nyet*

note записка *(f) zapiska*

notebook блокнот *(m) blaknot*

nothing ничего *nichivo*

novel повесть *(f) povis't'*

November ноябрь *(m) nayabr'*

now сейчас *sichyas*

nowadays в наши дни *v nashy dni*

nowhere нигде *nigdye*

number номер *(m) nomir*

nurse медсестра *(f) mitsistra*

O

obvious очевидный *achividny*

ocean океан *(m) akian*

o'clock: one o'clock один час *adin chyas;* **three o'clock** три часа *tri chisa*

October октябрь *(m) aktyabr'*

offer *(v)* предлагать/предложить *pridlagat'/pridlazhyt'*

often часто *chyasta*

oil масло *(n) masla*

ointment мазь *(f) mas'*

OK хорошо *Harasho*

old старый *stary;* **how old are you?** сколько тебе лет? *skol'ka tibye lyet?;* **old people** пожилые люди *pazhylyi lyoodi*

old town старый город *(m) stary gorat*

on на *na;* **it's on at ...** это идёт в ... *eta idyot v ...*

once однажды *adnazhdy;* **once a day/an hour** раз в день/в час *ras v dyen'/f chyas*

one один *adin*

only только *tol'ka*

open *(adj)* открытый *atkryty* **69**

open *(v)* открывать/открыть *atkryvat'/atkryt'*

operate оперировать *apiriravat'*

operation: to have an operation перенести операцию *pirinis'ti apiratsyyoo*

opinion мнение *(n) mnyeniye;* **in my opinion** по-моему *pa-moimoo*

opportunity возможность *(f) vazmozhnas't'*

opposite *(noun)* противоположность *(f) prativapalozhnas't'*

opposite *(prep)* напротив *naprotif*

optician оптик *(m) optik*

or или *ili*

orange апельсин *(m) apil'sin*

orchestra оркестр *(m) arkyestr*

order *(v)* заказывать/заказать *zakazyvat'/zakazat'* **47, 48**

order *(noun)* порядок *(m) paryadak;* **out of order** (закрыто на) ремонт *(zakryta na) rimont*

organic натуральный *natooral'ny*

organize организовывать *arganizovyvat'*

other другой *droogoï;* **others** другие *droogii*

otherwise иначе *inachi*

our наш *nash,* наша *nasha,* наше *nashe,* наши *nashy (see grammar)*

ours наш *nash,* наша *nasha,* наше *nashe,* наши *nashy (see grammar)*

outside наружу *naroozhoo,* снаружи *snaroozhy*

oven духовка *(f) dooHofka*

over: over there вон там *von tam*

overweight: my luggage is overweight у меня перевес багажа *oo minya pirivyes bagazha*

owe быть обязанным *byt' abyazanym* **51, 81**

own *(adj)* свой *svoï,* своя *svaya,* своё *svayo,* свои *svaï;* **my own car** моя машина *maya mashyna*

own *(v)* владеть *vladyet'*

owner владелец *(m) vladyelits*

pack собирать *sabirat'*; **to pack one's suitcase** собирать чемодан *sabirat' chimadan*

package holiday тур (m) *toor*

packed упакованный *oopakovany*

packet посылка (f) *pasylka*, упаковка (f) *oopakofka*

painting живопись (f) *zhyvapis'*

pair пара (f) *para*; **a pair of pyjamas** пижама (f) *pizhama*; **a pair of shorts** шорты (pl) *shorty*

palace дворец (m) *dvaryets*

pants трусы (pl) *troosy*

paper бумага (f) *boomaga*; **paper napkin** бумажная салфетка (f) *boomazhnaya salfyetka*; **paper tissue** бумажное полотенце (n) *boomazhnaye palatyentse*

parcel посылка (f) *pasylka*

pardon? простите? *prastiti?*

parents родители (mpl) *raditili*

park (noun) парк (m) *park*

park (v) парковаться/припарковаться *parkavatsa/priparkavatsa*

parking space место для парковки (n) *myesta dlya parkofki*

part часть (f) *chyas't'*; **to be a part of** быть частью *byt' chyas't'yoo*

party вечеринка (f) *vichirinka*

pass (noun) пропуск (m) *propoosk*

pass (v) проходить *praHadit'*

passenger пассажир (m) *pasazhyr*

passport паспорт (m) *paspart*

past мимо *mima*; **a quarter past ten** четверть одиннадцатого *chyetvirt' adinatsatava*

path тропинка (f) *trapinka* 75

patient пациент (m) *patsy-ent*

pay платить/заплатить *platit'/zaplatit'* 81, 82

pedestrian пешеход (m) *pishyHot*

pedestrianized street пешеходная улица (f) *pishyHodnaya oolitsa*

pee писать *pisat'*

pen ручка (f) *roochka*

pencil карандаш (m) *karandash*

people люди (pl) *lyoodi* 46

percent процент (m) *pratsent*

perfect отличный *atlichny*

perfume духи (pl) *dooHi*

perhaps возможно *vazmozhna*

period (menstrual) месячные (pl) *myesichnyi*

person человек (m) *chilavyek*, лицо (n) *litso*

personal stereo плеер (m) *pleir*

petrol бензин (m) *binzin*

petrol station заправка (f) *zaprafka*

phone (noun) телефон (m) *tilifon*

phone (v) звонить *zvanit*

phone box телефонная кабинка (f) *tilifonaya kabinka* 98

phone call звонок (m) *zvanok*; **to make a phone call** позвонить *pazvanit'*

phonecard телефонная карта (f) *tilifonaya karta* 98

phone number телефонный номер (m) *tilifony nomir*

photo фотография (f) *fatagrafiya*, снимок (m) *snimak*; **to take a photo of** сфотографировать что-либо *sfatagrafiravat' shto-liba* 87; **to take someone's photo** сфотографировать кого-либо *sfatagrafiravat' kavo-liba*

picnic пикник (m) *piknik*; **to have a picnic** устроить пикник *oostroit' piknik*

pie пирог (m) *pirok*

piece кусок (m) *koosok*; **a piece of** кусок (+ gen.) *koosok*; **a piece of fruit** кусочек фрукта *koosochik frookta*

piles геморрой (m) *gimaroі*

pillow подушка (f) *padooshka*

pillowcase наволочка (f) *navalachka*

pill таблетка (f) *tablyetka*; **to be on the pill** принимать противозачаточные таблетки *prinimat' prativazachyatachnyi tablyetki* 105

PIN (number) ПИН код (m) *pin kot*

pink розовый *rozavy*

pity: it's a pity стыдно *stydna*; **it's a pity that …** жалко, что … *zhalka, shto …*

place место (n) *myesta*

plan план (m) *plan*

plane самолет (m) *samalyot*

plant растение (n) *rastyeniye*

plaster (cast) гипс (m) *gips*

plastic пластмассовый *plastmasavy*

plastic bag полиэтиленовый пакет (m) *palitilyenavy pakyet* **81**

plate тарелка (f) *taryelka*

platform платформа (f) *platforma* **29**

play (noun) пьеса (f) *p'yesa*

play (v) играть/сыграть *igrat'/sygrat'*

please пожалуйста *pazhaloosta*

pleased довольный *davol'ny*; **pleased to meet you!** рад (m)/ рада (f) познакомиться *rat/rada paznakomitsa*

pleasure удовольствие (n) *oodavol'stviye*

plug (for bath) пробка (f) *propka*; (electrical) вилка (f) *vilka*

plug in включать/включить в сеть *fklyoochyat'/fklyoochit' f syet'*

plumber водопроводчик (m) *vadapravoochik*

point пункт (m) *poonkt*

Poland Польша (f) *Pol'sha*

Pole поляк (m) *palyak*, полька (f) *polyachka*

police милиция (f) *militsyya*, полиция (f) *palitsyya* **111**

policeman милиционер (m) *militsy-anyer*

police station отделение милиции (n) *adilyeniye militsyi* **110**

policewoman милиционер (m) *militsy-anyer*

poor бедный *byedny*

port порт (m) *port*

portrait портрет (m) *partryet*

Portuguese португальский *portoogal'ski*

possible возможный *vazmozhny*; **it's possible** возможно *vazmozhna*

post (noun) почта (f) *pochta*

postbox почтовый ящик (m) *pachtovy yaschik* **94**

postcard открытка (f) *atkrytka*

postcode почтовый код (m) *pachtovy kot*

poster плакат (m) *plakat*

poste restante до востребования *da vastryebyvaniya*

postman почтальон (m) *pachtal'yon*

post office почтовое отделение (n) *pachtovaye adilyeniye* **94**

pot кастрюля (f) *kastryoolya*

pound фунт (m) *foont*

powder пудра (f) *poodra*, порошок (m) *parashok*

practical практический *praktichiski*

pram коляска (f) *kalyaska*

prefer предпочитать *pridpachitat'*

pregnant беременный *biryeminy* **105**

prepare готовить/приготовить *gatovit'/prigatovit'*

prescription рецепт (m) *ritsept*

present подарок (m) *padarak* **86**

press пресса (f) *pryesa*

pressure давление (n) *davlyeniye*

previous предыдущий *pridydooschi*

price цена (f) *tsyna*

private частный *chyasny*

prize награда (f) *nagrada*

probably возможно *vazmozhna*

problem проблема (f) *prablyema*

procession шествие (n) *shestviye*

product продукт (m) *pradookt*

profession профессия (f) *prafyesiya*

programme программа (f) *pragrama*

promise обещать/пообещать *abischat'/paabischat'*

propose предлагать/предложить *pridlagat'/pridlazhyt'*

protect защищать/защитить *zaschischat'/zaschitit'*

public государственный *gasoodarstviny*; национальный *natsy-anal'ny*

public holiday официальный праздник (m) afitsy-al'ny praz'nik

pull тянуть tyanoot'; (sign on door) на себя na sibya

purple пурпурный poorpoorny

purpose: on purpose намеренно namyerina

purse кошелёк (m) kashylyok

push толкать talkat'; (sign on door) от себя at sibya

pushchair прогулочная коляска (m) pragoolachnaya kalyaska

put класть/положить klas't'/palazhyt'

put up with смириться с (+ inst.) smiritsa s

Q

quality качество (n) kachistva; **of good/bad quality** хорошего/плохого качества Haroshyva/plaHova kachistva

quarter четверть (f) chyetvirt'; **a quarter of an hour** четверть часа chyetvirt' chyasa; **a quarter to ten** без пятнадцати десять bis pitnatsati dyesit'

quay причал (m) prichyal

question вопрос (m) vapros

queue (noun) очередь (f) ochirit'

queue (v) стоять в очереди stayat' v ochiridi

quick быстрый bystry

quickly быстро bystra

quiet тихий tiHi

quite вполне vpalnye; **quite a lot of** довольно много davol'na mnoga

R

racist расист (m) rasist

racket ракетка (f) rakyetka

radiator радиатор (m) radiatar, обогреватель (m) abagrivatil'

radio радио (n) radia

radio station радиостанция (f) radiastantsyya

rain дождь (f) dosht'

rain (v) **it's raining** идёт дождь idyot dosht'

raincoat дождевик (m) dazhdivik

random: at random случайно sloochyaina, беспорядочно bisparyadachna

rape изнасилование (n) iznasilavaniye

rare редкий ryetki; (meat) с кровью s krov'yoo

rarely редко ryetka

rather скорее skaryeye, вернее vyirnyeye

raw сырой syroï

razor лезвие (n) lyezviye

razor blade бритвенное лезвие (n) britvinaya lyezviye

reach доходить daHadit'; (by phone) связываться svyazyvatsa

read читать/прочитать chitat'/prachitat'

ready готовый gatovy

reasonable рациональный ratsyanal'ny

receipt чек (m) chyek **82**

receive получать/получить paloochyat'/paloochit'

reception приёмная (f) priyomnaya, ресепшн (m) risepshn; **at reception** в приёмной v priyomnai

receptionist администратор (m) administratar

recognize узнавать/узнать ooznavat'/ooznat'

recommend рекомендовать rikamindavat' **39**, **45**, **47**

red красный krasny; (hair) рыжий ryzhy

red light красный свет (m) krasny svyet

reduce сокращать sakraschyat'

reduction скидка (f) skitka

red wine красное вино (n) krasnaye vino

refrigerator холодильник (m) Haladil'nik

refund (noun) компенсация (f) kampinsatsyya; **to get a refund** получить деньги назад paloochit' dyen'gi nazat

refund (v) возвращать/вернуть деньги vazvraschyat'/virnoot' dyen'gi

refuse отказывать/отказать *atkazyvat'/atkazat'*

registered зарегистрированный *zarigistrirovany*

registration number регистрационный номер *(m) rigistratsyony nomir*

remarkable замечательный *zamichatil'ny*

remember помнить *pomnit'*

remind напоминать/напомнить *napaminat'/napomnit'*

remove удалять/удалить *oodalyat'/ oodalit'*

rent (noun) аренда *(f) aryenda*, прокат *(m) prakat*

rent (v) арендовать *arindavat'*, сдавать в аренду *zdavat' v aryendoo* **41**

rental прокат *(m) prakat*

reopen вновь открывать *vnof' atkryvat'*

repair чинить *chinit'* **32**; **to get something repaired** отдать что-либо в ремонт *adat' shto-liba v rimont*

repeat повторять/повторить *pavtaryat'/pavtarit'* **10**

reserve бронировать *braniravat'* **38, 46**

reserved зарезервированный *zarizirvirovany*

rest (v) отдыхать/отдохнуть *adyHat'/ adaHnoot'*

rest (noun) **the rest** остаток *(m) astatak*

restaurant ресторан *(m) ristaran* **45**

return возвращаться/вернуться *vazvraschyatsa/virnootsa* **85**

return ticket обратный билет *(m) abratny bilyet*

reverse gear задняя передача *(f) zadniya piridachya*

reverse-charge call звонок за счет собеседника *(m) zvanok za schyot sabisyednika*

rheumatism ревматизм *(m) rivmatizm*

rib ребро *(n) ribro*

right (adj) правый *pravy*; прямой *primoi*

right (noun) право *(n) prava*; **to have the right to do something** быть вправе сделать что-либо *byt' vpravi z'dyelat' shto-liba*; **to the right (of)** направо от *naprava at*

right (adv) **right away** немедленно *nimyedlina*; **right beside** рядом с *(+ inst.) ryadam s*

ring кольцо *(n) kal'tso*

ripe спелый *spyely*

risk риск *(m) risk*

river река *(f) rika*

road дорога *(f) daroga*

road sign дорожный знак *(m) darozhny znak*

rock (stone) скала *(f) skala*

rollerblades роликовые коньки *(pl) rolikavyi kan'ki*

room комната *(f) komnata* **38, 39, 40**

rosé wine розовое вино *(n) rozavaye vino*

round вокруг *vakrook*

roundabout круговое движение *(n) kroogavoye dvizheniye*

rubbish мусор *(m) moosar*; **to take the rubbish out** выносить/вынести мусор *vynasit'/vynisti moosar*

rucksack рюкзак *(m) ryoogzak*

rug коврик *(m) kovrik*, плед *(m) plyet*

ruins развалины *(pl) razvaliny*; **in ruins** в развалинах *v razvalinaH*

run out кончиться *konchitsa*; **we've run out of petrol** у нас кончился бензин *oo nas konchilsya binzin*

S

sad грустный *groosny*

safe безопасный *bizapasny*

safety безопасность *(f) bizapasnas't'*

safety belt ремень безопасности *(m) rimyen' bizapasnas'ti*

sail парус *(m) paroos*

sailing парусный спорт (m) *paroosny sport*; **to go sailing** заниматься парусным спортом *zanimatsa paroosnym sportam*

sale продажа (f) *pradazha*; **for sale** продаётся *pradayotsa*; **in the sale** в продаже *f pradazhy*

sales распродажа (f) *raspradazha*

salt соль (f) *sol'*

salty солёный *salyony*

same такой же *takoï zhe*; **the same** то же самое *to zhe samaye* **50**

sand песок (m) *pisok*

sandals сандалии (pl) *sandalii*

sanitary towel прокладка (f) *praklatka*

Saturday суббота (f) *soobota*

saucepan кастрюля (f) *kastryoolya*

save (money) беречь *biryech'*; (person) спасать *spasat'*

say говорить *gavarit'*; **how do you say ...?** как будет ...? *kak boodit ...?*

scared напуганный *napoogany*; **to be scared of** бояться *bayatsa*

scenery пейзаж (m) *pizash*

scissors ножницы (pl) *nozhnitsy*

scoop: two scoops (of ice cream) два шарика *dva sharika*

scooter самокат (m) *samakat*

scotch скотч (m) *skoch*

Scotland Шотландия (f) *shatlandiya*

Scotsman шотландец (m) *shatlandits*

Scotswoman шотландка (f) *shatlantka*

Scottish шотландский *shatlanski*

scuba diving погружение с аквалангом (n) *pagroozheniye s akvalangam*

sea море (n) *mori*

seafood морепродукты (pl) *moripradookty*

seasick: I'm seasick меня укачивает *minya ookachivait*

seaside: at the seaside на побережье *na pabiryezh-i*

season время года (n) *vryemya goda*

seat место (n) *myesta* **24**

sea view вид на море (m) *vit na mori*

seaweed морская водоросль (f) *marskaya vodarasl'*

second второй *ftaroï*

second class второй класс (m) *ftaroï klas*

secondary school средняя школа (f) *sryednyaya shkola*

second-hand сэконд-хэнд *sekant-Hent*

secure безопасный *bizapasny*, надёжный *nadyozhny*

security безопасность (f) *bizapasnast'*

see видеть *vidit'*; **see you later!** до встречи! *da fstryechi!*; **see you soon!** до скорого! *da skorava!*; **see you tomorrow!** до завтра! *da zaftra!*

seem казаться *kazatsa*; **it seems that ...** кажется, что ... *kazhytsa, shto ...*

seldom редко *ryetka* **80**

sell продавать *pradavat'*

Sellotape® скотч (m) *skoch*

send посылать *pasylat'*

sender отправитель (m) *atpravitil'*

sense чувство (n) *choostva*

sensitive чувствительный *choostvitil'ny*

sentence предложение (n) *pridlazheniye*

separate отдельный *adyel'ny*

separately отдельно *adyel'na*

September сентябрь (m) *sintyabr'*

serious серёзный *sir'yozny*

several несколько *nyeskal'ka*

sex секс (m) *seks*; (gender) пол (m) *pol*

shade тень (f) *tyen'*; **in the shade** в тени *f tini*

shame: it's a shame стыдно *stydna*

shampoo шампунь (m) *shampoon'*

shape форма (f) *forma*

share делиться *dilitsa*

shave бриться *britsa*

shaving cream крем для бритья (m) *kryem dlya brit'ya*

shaving foam пена для бритья (f) *pyena dlya brit'ya*

she она *ana*

sheet лист (m) *list*

shellfish моллюск *(m) malyoosk*

shirt рубашка *(f) roobashka*

shock *(v)* поражать/поразить *parazhat'/paruzit'*

shocking скандальный *skandal'ny*

shoes обувь *(f) oboof*

shop магазин *(m) magazin*

shop assistant продавец *(m) pradavyets*, продавщица *(f) pradavshitsa*

shopkeeper владелец магазина *(m) vladyelits magazina*

shopping: to go shopping ходить по магазинам *hadit' pa magazinam*

shopping centre торговый центр *(m) targovy tsentr*

short низкий *nizki*; **I'm two ... short** мне не хватает двух ... *mnye ni hvatait dvooh ...*

short cut кратчайший путь *(m) krachyaïshi poot'*

shorts шорты *(pl) shorty*

short-sleeved с коротким рукавом *s korotkim rookavom*

shoulder плечо *(n) plichyo*

shout кричать/крикнуть *krichyat'/kriknoot'*

show *(noun)* шоу *sho-oo*, представление *(n) pritstavlyeniye* **62**

show *(v)* показывать/показать *pakazyvat'/pakazat'*

shower душ *(m) doosh*; **to have a shower** принимать/принять душ *prinimat'/prinyat' doosh*

shower gel гель для душа *(m) gyel' dlya doosha*

shut закрывать/закрыть *zakryvat'/zakryt'*

shuttle bus пригородный автобус *(m) prigarodny aftoboos*

shy застенчивый *zastyenchivy*

sick: to feel sick тошнить *tashnit'*; **I feel sick** меня тошнит *minya tashnit*

side сторона *(f) starana*

sign знак *(m) znak*

signal сигнал *(m) signal*

signature подпись *(f) potpis'*

silent тихий *tiHi*, безмолвный *bizmolvny*

silver серебряный *siryebryany*

silver-plated посеребрённый *pasiribryony*

since с тех пор (как) *s tyeH por (kak)*

sing петь *pyet'*

singer певец *(m) pivyets*, певица *(f) pivitsa*

single (man) холостой *Halastoï*; **(woman)** незамужняя *nizamoozhniya*

single (ticket) билет в один конец *(m) bilyet v adin kanyets*

sister сестра *(f) sistra*

sit down садиться/сесть *saditsa/syes't'*

size размер *(m) razmyer* **84**

ski boots лыжные ботинки *(pl) lyzhnyi batinki*

skiing лыжный спорт *(m) lyzhny sport*; **to go skiing** кататься на лыжах *katatsa na lyzhaH*

ski lift подъёмник *(m) pad-yomnik*

skin кожа *(f) kozha*

ski pole лыжная палка *(f) lyzhnaya palka*

ski resort лыжный курорт *(m) lyzhny koorort*

skirt юбка *(f) yoopka*

skis лыжи *(pl) lyzhy*

sky небо *(n) nyeba*

skyscraper небоскрёб *(m) nibaskryop*

sleep *(noun)* сон *(m) son*

sleep *(v)* спать *spat'*; **to sleep with** переспать с *(+ instr.) pirispat' s*

sleeping bag спальный мешок *(m) spal'ny mishok*

sleeping pill снотворное *(n) snatvornaye*

sleepy: to be sleepy хотеть спать *Hatyet' spat'*

sleeve рукав *(m) rookaf*

slice ломтик *(m) lomtik*

sliced нарезанный *naryezany*

slide слайд *(m) slaït*

slow медленный *myedliny*

slowly медленно *myedlina*

small маленький *malin'ki*

smell (noun) запах (m) zapaH

smell (v) пахнуть paHnoot'; **to smell good/bad** хорошо/плохо пахнуть Harasho/ploHa paHnoot'

smile (noun) улыбка (f) oolypka

smile (v) улыбаться/улыбнуться oolybatsa/oolybnootsa

smoke (v) курить koorit'

smoker курильщик (m) kooril'schik

snack закуска (f) zakooska

snow (noun) снег (m) snyek

snow (v) **it's snowing** идёт снег idyot snyek

so так tak; **so that** чтобы shtoby

soap мыло (n) myla

soccer футбол (m) footbol

socks носки (pl) naski

some некоторый nyekatary; **some people** некоторые nyekataryi

somebody, someone кто-нибудь kto-niboot', кто-то kto-ta

something что-нибудь shto-niboot', что-то shto-ta; **something else** что-то ещё sho-ta ischyo

sometimes иногда inagda

somewhere где-то gdye-ta; **somewhere else** где-то ещё gdye-ta ischyo

son сын (m) syn

song песня (f) pyesnya

soon скоро skora

sore больной bal'noï; **I have a sore throat** у меня болит горло oo minya balit gorla

sorry огорчённый agarchyony; **sorry!** извини(те)! izvini(ti)!

south юг (m) yook; **in the south** на юге na yoogi; **(to the) south of** к югу от k yoogoo at

souvenir сувенир (m) soovinir

Spain Испания (f) ispaniya

spare запасной zapasnoï

spare part запасная деталь (f) zapasnaya dital'

spare tyre запасная шина (f) zapasnaya shyna

spare wheel запасное колесо (n) zapasnoye kaliso

spark plug свеча зажигания (f) svicha zazhyganiya

speak говорить/сказать gavarit'/skazat' **9, 10, 99, 110**

special особый asoby; **today's special** блюдо дня (n) blyooda dnya

speciality фирменное блюдо (n) firminaye blyooda, местное блюдо (n) myesnaye blyooda **48**

speed скорость (f) skoras't'; **at full speed** на полном ходу na polnam Hadoo

spell писать pisat', диктовать по буквам diktavat' pa bookvam; **how do you spell it?** как это пишется? kak eta pishytsa?

spend проводить/провести pravadit'/pravisti

spice специя (f) spyetsyya

spicy острый ostry

spider паук (m) paook

splinter заноза (f) zanoza

split up расставаться/расстаться rastavatsa/rastatsa

spoil портить portit'

sponge губка (f) goopka

spoon ложка (f) loshka

sport спорт (m) sport

sports ground спортплощадка (f) sportplaschyatka

sporty спортивный spartivny

spot прыщик (m) pryschik

sprain: to sprain one's ankle вывихнуть лодыжку vyviHnoot' ladyshkoo

spring весна (f) visna

square площадь (f) ploschit'; **Red Square** Красная Площадь krasnaya ploschit'

stadium стадион (m) stadion

stain пятно (n) pitno

stairs лестница (f) lyesnitsa

stamp марка (f) marka **94**

start (v) начинать/начать nachinat'/nachyat'

state государство *(n) gasoodarstva*

statement утверждение *(n) ootvirzhdyeniye*

station станция *(f) stantsyya*

stay *(v)* оставаться/остаться *astavatsa/astatsa;* **to stay in touch** поддерживать общение *padyerzhyvat' apschyeniye*

stay *(n)* пребывание *(n) pribyvaniye*

steal красть/украсть *kras't'/ookras't'* **146**

step шаг *(m) shak*

sticking plaster пластырь *(m) plastyr'*

still water негазированная вода *(f) nigazirovanaya vada*

sting *(noun)* жало *(n) zhala*

sting *(v)* жалить/ужалить *zhalit'/oozhalit';* **to get stung by** быть ужаленным *(+ instr.) byt' oozhalinym* **104**

stock: out of stock нет в наличии *nyet v nalichii*

stomach живот *(m) zhyvot*

stone камень *(m) kamin'*

stop *(noun)* остановка *(f) astanofka* **30**

stop *(v)* останавливать/остановить *astanavlivat'/astanavit'*

stopcock запорный кран *(m) zaporny kran*

storey этаж *(m) etash*

storm буря *(f) boorya,* непогода *(f) nipagoda*

straight ahead, straight on прямо *pryama*

strange странный *strany*

street улица *(f) oolitsa*

strong сильный *sil'ny*

stuck застрявший *zastryafshy*

student студент *(m) stoodyent,* студентка *(f) stoodyentka* **23**

studies занятия *(pl) zanyatiya*

study изучать/изучить *izoochyat'/ izoochit';* **to study biology** изучать биологию *izoochyat' bialogiyoo*

style стиль *(m) stil'*

subtitled с субтитрами *s sooptitrami*

suburb окраина *(f) akraina*

suffer страдать *stradat'*

suggest предлагать *pridlagat'*

suit: does this suit me? мне это подходит? *mnye eta patHodit?*

suitcase чемодан *(m) chimadan* **25**

summer лето *(n) lyeta*

summit вершина *(f) virshyna*

sun солнце *(n) sontse;* **in the sun** на солнце *na sontse*

sunbathe загорать *zagarat'*

sunburnt: to get sunburnt обгореть *abgaryet'*

sun cream крем для загара *(m) kryem dlya zagara*

Sunday воскресение *(n) vaskrisyeniye*

sunglasses солнечные очки *(pl) solnichnyi achki*

sunhat панама *(f) panama*

sunrise восход *(m) vasHot*

sunset закат *(m) zakat*

sunstroke солнечный удар *(m) solnichny oodar;* **to get sunstroke** получить солнечный удар *paloochit' solnichny oodar*

supermarket супермаркет *(m) soopirmarkit* **42, 80**

supplement приложение *(n) prilazheniye*

sure уверенный *oovyeriny*

surgical spirit хирургический спирт *(m) Hiroorgichiski spirt*

surname фамилия *(f) familiya*

surprise *(noun)* сюрприз *(m) syoorpris*

surprise *(v)* удивлять/удивить *oodivlyat'/oodivit'*

sweat пот *(m) pot*

sweater свитер *(m) svityr*

sweet *(adj)* сладкий *slatki*

sweet *(noun)* конфета *(f) kanfyeta*

swim *(noun)* **to go for a swim** купаться/выкупаться *koopatsa/ vykoopatsa*

swim *(v)* плавать *plavat'*

swimming плавание *(n) plavaniye*

swimming pool бассейн *(m) basyein*

swimming trunks плавки *(pl) plafki*

swimsuit купальный костюм *(m) koopal'ny kastyoom*

switchboard operator телефонист *(m) tilifanist*, телефонистка *(f) tilifanistka*

switch off выключать/выключить *vyklyoochyat'/vyklyoochit'*

switch on включать/включить *fklyoochyat'/fklyoochit'*

swollen: my finger is swollen у меня палец опух *oo minya palits apooH*

synagogue синагога *(f) sinagoga*

syrup сироп *(m) sirop*

T

table стол *(m) stol* **46**

tablespoon столовая ложка *(f) stalovaya loshka*

tablet таблетка *(f) tablyetka*

take брать/взять *brat'/vzyat'*; **it takes two hours** длится два часа *dlitsa dva chisa*

takeaway на вынос *na vynas*

take off *(plane)* взлетать/взлететь *vzlitat'/vzlityet*

talk говорить *gavarit'*

tall высокий *vysoki*

tampon тампон *(m) tampon*

tap кран *(m) kran*

taste *(noun)* вкус *(m) fkoos*

taste *(v)* пробовать/попробовать *probavat'/paprobavat'*

tax налог *(m) nalok*

tax-free не облагаемый налогом *ni ablagaimy nalogam*

taxi такси *(n) taksi* **33**

taxi driver таксист *(m) taksist*

team команда *(f) kamanda*

teaspoon чайная ложка *(f) chyainaya loshka*

teenager подросток *(m) padrostak*

telephone *(noun)* телефон *(m) tilifon*

telephone *(v)* звонить по телефону *zvanit' pa tilifonoo*

telephone call звонок *(m) zvanok*

television телевизор *(m) tilivizar*

tell говорить/сказать *gavarit'/skazat'*

temperature температура *(f) timpiratoora*; **to take one's temperature** мерить/померить температуру *(+ dat.) myerit'/pamyerit' timpiratooroo*

temple храм *(m) Hram*

temporary временный *vryeminy*

tennis теннис *(m) tenis*

tennis court теннисный корт *(m) tenisny kort*

tennis shoes теннисные туфли *(pl) tenisnyi toofli*

tent палатка *(f) palatka*

tent peg колышек от палатки *(m) kolyshek at palatki*

terminal конечная станция *(f) kanyechnaya stantsyya*

terrace терраса *(f) tirasa*

terrible ужасный *oozhasny*

thanks спасибо *spasiba*; **thanks to** спасибо *(+ dat.) spasiba*

thank you спасибо вам *spasiba vam*; **thank you very much** большое вам спасибо *bal'shoye vam spasiba*

that тот *(m) tot*; **that one** вот тот *vot tot*

the *(see grammar)*

theatre театр *(m) tiatr*

theft кража *(f) krazha*

their их *iH*

theirs их *iH*

them их *iH*, им *im*, ими *imi (see grammar)*

theme park парк отдыха *(m) park otdyHa*

then тогда *tagda*, потом *patom*

there там *tam*; **there is ...** это ... *eta ...*, вот... *vot*; **there are ...** это... *eta ...*, вот... *vot*

therefore поэтому *paetamoo*

thermometer градусник *(m) gradoosnik*

Thermos® flask термос *(m) termas*

these эти *eti*; **these ones** вот эти *vot eti*

---

they они *ani*; **they say that …** говорят, что … *gavaryat, shto …*

thief вор *(m) vor*

thigh бедро *(n) bidro*

thin худой *Hoodoï*

thing вещь *(f) vyeschi*; **things** вещи *vyeschi*

think думать/подумать *doomat'/padoomat'*

think about обдумывать/обдумать *abdoomyvat'/abdoomat'*

thirst жажда *(f) zhazhda*

thirsty: to be thirsty хотеть пить *Hatyet' pit'*

this этот *etat*; **this one** вот этот *vot etat*; **this evening** сегодня вечером *sivodnya vyechiram*; **this is …** это … *eta …*

those те *tye*; **those ones** вот те *vot tye*

throat горло *(n) gorla*

throw кидать/кинуть *kidat'/kinoot'*

throw out выкидывать/выкинуть *vykidyvat'/vykinoot'*

Thursday четверг *(m) chitvyerk*

ticket билет *(m) bilyet* **23, 24, 63**

ticket office касса *(f) kasa* **67**

tidy опрятный *apryatny*, чистый *chisty*

tie галстук *(m) galstook*

tight узкий *oozki*, тесный *tyesny*

tights колготки *(pl) kalgotki*

time время *(n) vryemya* **118**; **what time is it?** сколько времени? *skol'ka vryemini?*; **from time to time** время от времени *vryemya za vryemini*; **on time** вовремя *vovrimya*; **three/four times** три/четыре раза *tri/chityri raza*

time difference разница во времени *(f) raznitsa va vryemini*

timetable расписание *(n) raspisaniye* **23**

tinfoil фольга *(f) fal'ga*

tip чаевые *(pl) chiivyi*

tired уставший *oostafshy*

tobacco табак *(m) tabak*

tobacconist's табачный киоск *(m) tabachny kiosk*

today сегодня *sivodnya*

together вместе *vmyes'ti*

toilet туалет *(m) tooalyet* **9, 46**

toilet bag косметичка *(f) kasmitichka*

toilet paper туалетная бумага *(f) tooalyetnaya boomaga*

toiletries туалетные принадлежности *(pl) tooalyetnyye prinadlyezhnasti*

toll сбор *(m) zbor*

tomorrow завтра *zaftra*; **tomorrow evening** завтра вечером *zaftra vyechiram*; **tomorrow morning** завтра утром *zaftra ootram*

tongue язык *(m) yizyk*

tonight сегодня вечером *sivodnya vyechiram*

too слишком *slishkam*; **too bad** слишком плохо *slishkam ploHa*; **too many/too much** слишком много *slishkam mnoga*

tooth зуб *(m) zoop*

toothbrush зубная щётка *(f) zoobnaya schyotka*

toothpaste зубная паста *(f) zoobnaya pasta*

top вершина *(f) virshyna*; **at the top** на вершине *na virshyni*

torch фонарь *(m) fanar'*

touch касаться/коснуться *kasatsa/kasnootsa*

tourism туризм *(m) toorizm*

tourist турист *(m) toorist*

tourist office экскурсионное бюро *(n) ikskoorsionaye byooro* **67**

tourist trap приманка для туристов *(f) primanka dlya tooristaf*

towel полотенце *(n) palatyentse*

town город *(m) gorat*

town centre центр города *(m) tsentr gorada*

town hall городская администрация *(f) garatskaya administratsyya*

toy игрушка *(f) igrooshka*

traditional традиционный *traditsy-ony*

traffic транспорт *(m)* *transport*

traffic jam пробка *(f)* *propka*

train поезд *(m)* *poist* **29; the train to Moscow** поезд до Москвы *poist da maskvy*

train station вокзал *(m)* *vagzal*

tram трамвай *(m)* *tramvaï*

transfer *(money)* переводить/перевести *pirivadit'/pirivisti* **91**

translate переводить/перевести *pirivadit'/pirivisti*

travel *(v)* путешествовать *pootishestvavat'*

travel agency турбюро *(n)* *toorbyooro*

traveller's cheque дорожный чек *(m)* *darozhny chyek*

trip поездка *(f)* *payestka;* **have a good trip!** счастливого пути! *schislivava pooti!*

trolleybus троллейбус *(m)* *tralyeïboos*

trousers брюки *(pl)* *bryooki*

true правда *pravda*

try пробовать/попробовать *probavat'/paprobavat';* **to try to do something** попробовать сделать что-то *probavat'/paprobavat' z'dyelat' shto-to*

try on примерять/примерить *primiryat'/primyerit'* **84**

tube *(underground)* метро *(n)* *mitro*

tube station станция метро *(f)* *stantsyya mitro*

Tuesday вторник *(m)* *ftornik*

turn *(noun)* **it's your turn** сейчас ваша очередь *sichyas vasha ochirit'*

turn *(v)* поворачивать/повернуть *pavarachivat'/povirnoot'*

twice дважды *dvazhdy*

type *(kind)* тип *(m)* *tip*

typical типичный *tipichny*

tyre шина *(f)* *shyna*

U

Ukraine Украина *(f)* *OOkraina*

Ukrainian *(adj)* украинский *ookrainki*

Ukrainian *(noun)* украинец *(m)* *ookrainits,* украинка *(f)* *ookrainka*

umbrella зонтик *(m)* *zontik*

uncle дядя *(m)* *dyadya*

uncomfortable неудобный *nioodobny*

under под *pod*

underground *(noun)* метро *(n)* *mitro* **28**

underground line линия метро *(f)* *liniya mitro*

underground station станция метро *(f)* *stantsyya mitro* **29**

underneath под *pod,* внизу *vnizoo*

understand понимать/понять *panimat'/panyat'* **10**

underwear нижнее бельё *(n)* *nizhniye bil'yo*

United Kingdom Великобритания *(f)* *vilikabritaniya*

United States Соединённые Штаты *(pl)* *saidinyonyi shtaty*

until до *do*

upset расстроенный *rastroiny*

upstairs вверх по лестнице *vyerH pa lesnitsy*

urgent срочный *srochny*

us нас *nas,* нам *nam,* нами *nami* (see grammar)

use использовать *ispol'zavat';* **to be used for** использоваться для *(+ gen.) ispol'zavat'sa dlya;* **I'm used to it** я привык к этому *ya privyk k etamoo*

useful полезный *palyezny*

useless бесполезный *bispalyezny*

usually обычно *abychna*

U-turn разворот *(m)* *razvarot*

V

vaccinate against прививать против *(+ gen.) privivat' protif*

valid действительный *diïstvitil'ny;* **valid for** действителен в течение *diïstvitilyen v tichyenii*

valley долина *(f)* *dalina*

VAT НДС *en-de-es*

vegetarian вегетарианец *(m)* *vigitrianits,* вегетарианка *(f)* *vigitarianka*

very очень *ochin'*

view вид (m) *vit*

villa вилла (f) *vila*

village деревня (f) *diryevnya*

visa виза (f) *viza*

visit (noun) посещение (n) *pasischyeniye*, визит (m) *vizit*

visit (v) посещать/посетить *pasischyat'/ pasitit*

volleyball волейбол (m) *valibol*

vomit (noun) рвота (f) *rvota*

vomit (v) рвать/вырвать *rvat'/vyrvat'*

waist талия (f) *taliya*

wait ждать *zhdat'*; **to wait for somebody/something** ждать кого-нибудь/чего-нибудь *zhdat' kavo-niboot'/chivo-niboot'*

waiter официант (m) *afitsy-ant*

waitress официантка (f) *afitsy-antka*

wake up будить *boodit'*

Wales Уэльс (m) *ooel's*

walk (noun) прогулка (f) *pragoolka*; **to go for a walk** гулять *goolyat*

walking boots туристическая обувь (f) *tooristichiskaya oboof'*

Walkman® плеер (m) *pleir*

wallet бумажник (m) *boomazhnik*

want хотеть *Hatyet'*; **to want to do something** хотеть сделать что-либо *Hatyet' z'dyelat' shto-liba*

warm тёплый *tyoply*

warn предупреждать *pridooprizhdat'*

wash мыть *myt'*; **to wash one's hair** мыть/помыть голову *myt'/pamyt' golavoo*

washbasin таз (m) *tas*

washing стирка (f) *stirka*; **to do the washing** стирать/постирать *stirat'/ pastirat'*

washing machine стиральная машина (f) *stiral'naya mashyna*

washing powder стиральный порошок (m) *stiral'ny parashok*

washing-up liquid жидкость для мытья посуды (f) *zhytkast' dlya myt'ya pasoody*

wasp оса (f) *asa*

waste тратить/потратить *tratit'/ patratit'*

watch (noun) часы (mpl) *chisy*

watch (v) смотреть *smatryet'*; **watch out!** осторожно! *astarozhna!*

water вода (f) *vada* 48, 49

water heater кипятильник (m) *kipitil'nik*

waterproof водостойкий *vadastoiki*

waterskis водные лыжи (pl) *vodnyi lyzhy*

wave волна (f) *valna*

way путь (m) *poot'*

way in вход (m) *fHot*

way out выход (m) *vyHat*

we мы *my*

weak слабый *slaby*

wear носить *nasit'*

weather погода (f) *pagoda*; **the weather's bad** погода плохая *pagoda plaHaya*

weather forecast прогноз погоды (m) *pragnos pagody* 20

website сайт (m) *saît*

Wednesday среда (f) *srida*

week неделя (f) *nidyelya*

weekend выходные (mpl) *vyHadnyi*

welcome добро пожаловать *dabro pazhalavat*; **you're welcome** пожалуйста *pazhaloosta*

well хорошо *Harasho*; **I'm very well** у меня всё хорошо *oo minya fsyo Harasho*; **well done** (meat) хорошо приготовленный *Harasho prigatovliny*

well-known известный *izvyesny*

Welsh уэльский *ooel'ski*

Welshman валлиец (m) *valiyets*

Welshwoman валийка (f) *valika*

west запад (m) *zapat*; **in the west** на западе *na zapadi*; **(to the) west of** на западе от (+ gen.) *na zapadi at*

wet мокрый *mokry*

wetsuit гидрокостюм *(m)* gidrakastyoom

what что shto; **what do you want?** что вы хотите? shto vy Hatiti?

wheel колесо *(n)* kaliso

wheelchair инвалидное кресло *(n)* invalidnaye kryesla

when когда kagda

where где gdye; **where is/are ...?** где находится/находятся ...? gdye naHoditsa/naHodyatsa ...?; **where are you from?** откуда вы? atkooda vy?; **where are you going?** куда вы собираетесь? kooda vy sabiraitis'?

which который katory

while пока paka

white белый byely

white wine белое вино *(n)* byelaye vino

who кто kto; **who's calling?** кто говорит? kto gavarit?

whole целый tsely; **the whole cake** весь пирог vyes' pirok

whose чей chyeï, чья chya, чьё chyo

why почему pachimoo

wide широкий shyroki

wife жена *(f)* zhyna

wild дикий diki

wind ветер *(m)* vyetir

window окно *(n)* akno; **in the window** в окне v aknye

windscreen ветровое стекло *(n)* vitravoye stiklo

windsurfing виндсёрфинг *(m)* vindsyorfink

wine вино *(n)* vino **48**, **50**

winter зима *(f)* zima

with вместе с (+ inst.) vmyesti s

withdraw снимать/снять snimat'/ snyat'

without без biz

woman женщина *(f)* zhenschina

wonderful чудесный choodyesny

wood дерево *(n)* dyeriva

wool шерсть *(f)* sherst'

work *(noun)* работа *(f)* rabota; **work of art** произведение искусства praizvidyeniye iskoostva

work *(v)* работать rabotat' **15**

works завод *(m)* zavot

world мир *(m)* mir

worse хуже Hoozhe; **to get worse** ухудшиться ooHootshytsa; **it's worse than ...** это хуже, чем ... eta Hoozhe, chyem ...

wound рана *(f)* rana

wrist запястье *(n)* zapyas't'ye

write писать pisat' **11**, **82**

wrong неправильный nipravil'ny

XYZ

X-rays рентген *(m)* ringyen

year год *(m)* got

yellow жёлтый zholty

yes да da

yesterday вчера fchira; **yesterday evening** вчера вечером fchira vyechiram

you *(informal)* ты ty; *(formal)* вы vy

young молодой maladoï

your *(informal)* твой tvoï; *(formal)* ваш vash

yours *(informal)* твой tvoï; *(formal)* ваш vash

youth hostel молодёжная турбаза *(f)* maladyozhnaya toorbaza

zero ноль *(m)* nol'

zip молния *(f)* molniya

zoo зоопарк *(m)* zaapark

zoom (lens) зум *(m)* zoom

DICTIONARY

RUSSIAN-ENGLISH

Аа

аварийный выход emergency exit
август August
авиалиния airline
авиапочта airmail
автобус bus, coach
автобусная остановка bus stop
автобусный маршрут bus route
автовокзал bus station
автоответчик answering machine
автосервис breakdown service
автостоп hitchhiking
автостоянка car park
автострада motorway
адаптер adaptor
адвокат lawyer
адрес address
акклиматизация jetlag
алкоголь alcohol
аллергический allergic
альпинизм climbing
американец American (m)
американка American (f)
американский American (adj)
английский English (adj)
англичанин Englishman
англичанка Englishwoman
Англия England
антибиотик antibiotics
апельсин orange
аппендицит appendicitis
апрель April
аптека chemist's
аренда rental, hire
арендовать to rent, to hire
аспирин aspirin

ассортимент stock
астма asthma
аэропорт airport

Бб

багаж luggage; **у меня перевес багажа** my luggage is overweight
багажник car boot
байдарка kayak
бакалея grocer's
балкон balcony
бампер bumper
банк bank
банка can, tin
бар bar
барбекю barbecue
бассейн swimming pool
батарея battery
бег трусцой jogging
бедный poor
бедро hip, thigh
без without; **без пятнадцати десять** a quarter to ten
безмолвный silent
безопасность safety, security
безопасный safe, secure
белое вино white wine
белый white
бельгиец Belgian (m)
бельгийка Belgian (f)
бельгийский Belgian (adj)
Бельгия Belgium
бензин petrol
берег river bank, coast
беременный pregnant
беречь to save money

бесплатный free of charge
беспокоить to disturb
бесполезный useless
беспорядочный disorderly, random
бессонница insomnia
библиотека library
билет ticket
билет в один конец single ticket
бинокль binoculars
бинт bandage
ближайший nearest
блокнот notebook
блюдо dish; **фирменное блюдо** speciality dish; **местное блюдо** local speciality; **блюдо дня** dish of the day
болезнь illness
болеть to hurt
больница hospital
больной ill
больше more; **больше нет** there's no more; **больше, чем** more than
большинство most; **большинство людей** most people
большой big
борода beard
ботанический сад botanical garden
ботинок boot *(footwear)*
бояться to be afraid
брат brother
брать/взять to take; **брать в прокат** to hire; **брать напрокат** to borrow
бритвенное лезвие razor blade
бриться to shave
бронирование booking, reservation
бронировать/забронировать to book
бронхит bronchitis
брошюра brochure
брюки trousers
будильник alarm clock
будить to wake up
будь(те) здоровы! bless you!
буёк buoy
булочная baker's, bakery
бумага paper

бумажная салфетка paper napkin
бумажник wallet
бумажное полотенце paper tissue
буря storm
бутылка bottle
бывший former
быстро quickly
быстрорастворимый кофе instant coffee
быстрый fast
быть to be; **быть в хорошем/плохом настроении** to be in a good/bad mood; **быть обязанным** to owe; **быть похожим** to look like
бюстгальтер bra

Вв

в in, at; **в Англии** in England; **в 2007 году** in 2007; **в девятнадцатом веке** in the 19th century; **в течение часа** in an hour
важный important
валлиец Welshman
валийка Welshwoman
валюта currency
ванна bath
ванная bathroom
ванное полотенце bath towel
вата cotton wool
ваш your, yours
Ваше здоровье! cheers!
вверх по лестнице upstairs
вдвоём both; **мы вдвоём** both of us
вегетарианец vegetarian *(m)*
вегетарианка vegetarian *(f)*
везде everywhere
век century
великий great
Великобритания Great Britain
велосипед bicycle
велосипедная cycle path
верить/поверить to believe
вернее rather
вершина summit
весна spring

вести машину to drive a car

весь/вся /всё/все all; **всю неделю** all week; **всё равно** all the same; **всё время** all the time; **всё включено** all inclusive

ветер wind

ветровое стекло windscreen

вечер evening; **вечером** in the evening

вечеринка party

вешалка coathanger

вещь thing

вздремнуть to take a nap

взлетать/взлететь to take off *(plane)*

взрыв explosion

взрываться to burst

вид view; **вид на море** sea view

видеть to see

виза visa

визит visit

вилка plug *(electrical)*

вилка fork

вилла villa

виндсёрфинг windsurfing

вино wine

включать/включить to switch on; **включать/включить в сеть** to plug in

включён included

вкус taste

вкусно tasty

владелец owner

владеть to own

влажный damp

вместе together; **вместе с** together with

вместо instead of

вниз по лестнице downstairs

внизу below, downstairs

внизу underneath

вновь again

внутри inside

вода water

вода из-под крана non-drinking water

водительские права driving licence

водные лыжи waterskis

водопроводчик plumber

водостойкий waterproof

возвращать/вернуть to give back; **возвращать/вернуть деньги** to refund; **возвращаться/вернуться** to return, to come back

возможно perhaps, probably

возможность opportunity, possibility

возраст age

вокзал train station

вокруг around

волдырь blister

волейбол volleyball

волна wave *(in sea)*

волосы hair

вон там over there

вопрос question

вор thief

ворота gate

воскресение Sunday

восток east; **на востоке** in the east; **к востоку от** to the east of

востребования: до востребования poste restante

восход sunrise

вот here is/are; **вот...** there is/are...

вперёд forwards

впереди in front of

вполне quite, completely

вправе right; **быть вправе сделать что-либо** to have the right to do something

врач doctor

временный temporary

время time; **сколько времени?** what time is it?; **время от времени** from time to time; **вовремя** on time; **время года** season; **время закрытия** closing time

все everyone

всё everything; **всё же** still

всегда always

вспышка flash

вставать/встать to get up

встреча meeting

встречать(ся) to meet
всюду everywhere
всякий: на всякий случай just in case
вторая половина дня afternoon
вторник Tuesday
второй second: **второй класс** second class; **второй этаж** first floor
вход entrance
входить/войти to come/go in
входной билет admission ticket
вчера yesterday; **вчера вечером** yesterday evening
вы you
вывихнуть лодыжку to sprain one's ankle
выглядеть to look; **выглядеть усталым** to look tired
выкидывать/выкинуть to throw out
выключать/выключить to switch off
вынос: на вынос takeaway
выпить to have a drink; **пойти выпить** to go for a drink
высокий high, tall
высокое давление high blood pressure
выставка exhibition
выхлопная труба exhaust pipe
выход exit, way out
выходить/выйти to go out
выходной holiday, day off; **на выходных** at the weekend, on holiday
выше above

Гг

газ gas
газета newspaper
газетный киоск newspaper kiosk
газированный fizzy
газовый баллон gas cylinder
галерея gallery
галстук tie
гараж garage

гарантировать to guarantee
гарантия guarantee
гардероб cloakroom
где where; **где находится/ находятся ...?** where is/are ...?
где-то somewhere; **где-то ещё** somewhere else
гель для душа shower gel
геморрой piles
Германия Germany
гидрокостюм wetsuit
гинеколог gynaecologist
гипс plaster (cast)
главный main; **главное блюдо** main course
гладить/погладить to iron
глаз eye
глубокий deep
глухой deaf
говорить/сказать to talk, to say, to tell
год year
годовщина anniversary
Голландия Holland
голова head; **у меня болит голова** I have a headache
голод hunger
голубой light blue
гольф golf
гомосексуалист homosexual (m)
гора mountain
гордиться to be proud of
гореть/сгореть to burn
горло throat
горная хижина mountain hut
горный велосипед mountain bike
город city, town
городская администрация town hall
горячий hot: **горячее блюдо** hot dish; **горячий шоколад** hot chocolate
господин Mr
госпожа Mrs
гостиная living room
гостиница hotel

гость guest
государственный public, state *(adj)*
государство state
готовить/приготовить to cook, to prepare
готовка cooking
готовый ready
градус degree *(temperature)*
градусник thermometer
граммы grams
границей: за границей abroad
границу: за границу abroad
Греция Greece
грипп flu
громкий loud
грудная клетка chest
грузовик lorry
грустный sad
грязный dirty
губа lip
губка sponge
гулять to go for a walk

Дд

да yes
давать/дать to give
давление pressure
далеко far; **далеко от** far from
дамская сумочка handbag
дата рождения date of birth
дважды twice
дверь door
двигатель engine
движение в оба конца shuttle
дворец palace
дебетовая карта debit card
девичья фамилия maiden name
девушка girl, girlfriend
дежурная аптека duty chemist's
дезинфицировать to disinfect
дезодорант deodorant
действительный valid; **действителен в течение** valid for
декабрь December

декларировать/задекларировать to declare
делать покупки to go shopping
делать/сделать to do, to make
деликатес deli
делиться to share
день day; **день рождения** birthday;
деньги money
деревня village
дерево wood
держать to hold
десерт dessert
детская бутылочка baby's bottle
дешёвый cheap
диабет diabetes
диета diet; **сидеть на диете** to be on a diet
дизельный diesel
дикий wild
диктовать по буквам to spell
дискотека disco
длинный long
длится дьа часа it lasts two hours
длиться to last
для for
для того, чтобы so that
дни: в наши дни nowadays
дно bottom; **на дне** at the bottom of
до until, before; **до сих пор** still, until now; **до встречи!** see you later!;
до завтра! see you tomorrow!; **до свидания** goodbye; **до скорого!** see you soon!
добро пожаловать welcome
добрый good; **доброе утро** good morning; **добрый день** good afternoon; **добрый вечер** good evening
довольно много quite a lot
довольно pleased
договариваться/договориться to arrange; **договариваться/договориться о встрече** to arrange to meet
дождевик raincoat
дождь rain

документы identity papers
долгое время a long time
должен to have to; **сейчас, должно быть, пять часов** it must be 5 o'clock; **я должен идти** I must go
долина valley
дом house; **дом отдыха** holiday camp
дома at home; **возвращаться домой** to go home
домик для гостей guest house
дополнительно extra
дорога road
дорогой dear, expensive
дорожный road *(adj)*; **дорожный знак** road sign; **дорожный чек** traveller's cheque
доска для сёрфинга surfboard
достаточно enough
доступ access
доступный available
доходить to reach
дочь daughter
драка fight
дремота nap
друг friend *(m)*
другой another, other; **другие** others
думать/подумать to think
духи perfume
духовка oven
душ shower
дымоход chimney
дядя uncle

Ее

Европа Europe
европейский European
его his, him
еда food
единица item
её hers, her
ему him
если if
есть to eat
ехать to go by transport
ещё нет not yet

Жж

жажда thirst
жалить to sting; **быть ужаленным** to get stung
жалко it's a pity
жало sting
жаловаться/пожаловаться to complain
жалость pity
жара heat
жареный fried
жарить to fry
жаркий hot; **жарко** it's hot *(weather)*
ждать to wait; **ждать кого-нибудь/чего-нибудь** to wait for somebody/something
жёлтый yellow
желудочный грипп gastric flu
жена wife
женатый married
жених fiancé
женский туалет ladies' toilet
женщина woman
жёсткий hard
живой alive
живопись painting
живот stomach
животное animal
жидкость для мытья посуды washing-up liquid
жизнь life
жирный fat, fatty
жить to live; **жить за границей** to live abroad
журнал magazine

Зз

за behind
заблудиться to get lost; **я заблудился/заблудилась** I'm lost
заболевать/заболеть to fall ill
завод factory, works
завтра tomorrow; **завтра вечером**

tomorrow evening; **завтра утром** tomorrow morning
завтрак breakfast
завтракать to have breakfast
задать вопрос to ask a question
задержанный delayed
задержка delay
задняя передача reverse gear
зажигалка lighter
зажигать/зажечь to light
заказывать/заказать to order
заканчивать/закончить to finish
закат sunset
закрывать/закрыть to close, to shut
закрыто на ремонт out of order
закрытый closed
закуска snack, starter
залог deposit
замечательный remarkable
замок castle
замужем married
заниматься to do (a sport); **заниматься подводным плаванием** to go diving
заноза splinter
занятия studies
занятый busy
запад west; **на западе** in the west; **на западе от** to the west of
запасной spare; **запасная деталь** spare part; **запасная шина** spare tyre; **запасное колесо** spare wheel
запах smell, flavour
запирать/запереть to lock
записка note
заполнять/заполнить to fill in
запор constipation
запорный кран stopcock
заправка petrol station
заправлять/заправить бензином to fill up with petrol
запрещённый forbidden
запястье wrist
заразный contagious
заранее in advance
зарегистрированный registered

зарезервированный reserved
застенчивый shy
застрявший stuck
засыпать/заснуть to fall asleep
защищать/защитить to protect
звать to call
звонить/позвонить to phone
звонок telephone call; **звонок за счет собеседника** reverse-charge call
здание building
здесь here
здоровье health
здравствуй(те) hello
зелёный green
земля earth, ground; **на земле** on the ground
зеркало mirror
зима winter
знак sign
знать to know; **я не знаю** I don't know
значить to mean; **что значит …?** what does … mean?
зонтик umbrella
зоопарк zoo
зуб tooth
зубная паста toothpaste
зубная щётка toothbrush
зум zoom (lens)

Ии

и and
игра game
играть/сыграть to play
игрушка toy
идёт дождь it's raining
идёт снег it's snowing
идти to go on foot
из from
избыток excess
известный well-known
извинение excuse
извинить to excuse; **извини(те)!** sorry!, excuse me!

из-за because of
излишек excess
изменение change
изнасилование rape
изучать/изучить to study
или or
им him
им/ими them
иметь to have
имя first name
иначе otherwise
инвалид disabled person
инвалидное кресло wheelchair
иногда sometimes
иностранец foreigner (m)
иностранка foreigner (f)
иностранный foreign
интернет Internet; **интернет кафе** Internet café
инфекция infection
информация information
Ирландия Ireland
ирландский Irish
искать to look for
исключением: за исключением except
исключительный exceptional
искусство art
Испания Spain
использовать to use
исчерпывать to exhaust, to wear out
Италия Italy
итальянский Italian
их their, theirs
июль July
июнь June

Кк

каждый each; **каждый день** every day
казаться to seem; **кажется, что ...** it seems that ...
как as; **как дела?** how are you?; **как можно раньше** as soon as possible;
как будет ...? how do you say ...?; **какой ...?** what kind of ...?
камень stone
камера хранения left-luggage (office)
капли drops
карандаш pencil
карта map
карточка card
касаться/коснуться to touch
каска helmet
касса cashpoint, checkout, ticket office
кастрюля saucepan
кататься на лыжах to ski
кафе café
качество quality; **хорошего/плохого качества** of good/bad quality
кашель cough
кашлять to have a cough
квартира flat, apartment
кемпинг camping, campsite
кидать/кинуть to throw
километр kilometre
кино cinema
кипятильник water heater
кладбище cemetery
класть/положить to put
климат climate
ключ key
книга book
книжный магазин bookshop
коврик rug
когда when
код code
кожа skin
кожица peel
кола Coke®
колготки tights
колено knee
колесо wheel
коллекция collection
колышек от палатки tent peg
кольцо ring
коляска pram
команда team
комар mosquito

комната room
компания company
компенсация refund
комплексная страховка
  comprehensive insurance
компьютер computer
комфортабельный comfortable
конверт envelope
кондиционер air conditioning
конец end; **в конце улицы** at the
  end of the street
конечная станция terminal
конечно of course
консульство consulate
контакт contact
контактные линзы contact lenses
конфета sweet
концерт concert
концертный зал concert hall
кончиться to run out
коричневый brown
коробка передач gearbox
коротким: с коротким рукавом
  short-sleeved
косметичка toilet bag
который which
кофе coffee
кошелёк purse
кража theft
кран tap
красивый beautiful
красный red; **красное вино** red
  wine; **красный свет** red light
красть/украсть to steal
кратчайший путь short cut
кредитная карта credit card
крем cream: **крем для бритья**
  shaving cream; **крем для загара** sun
  cream; **крем после загара** after-sun
  cream
крест cross
кричать/крикнуть to shout
кровать bed
кровоточить to bleed
кровь blood; **с кровью** rare *(meat)*
кровяное давление blood pressure

круговое движение roundabout
круиз cruise
крутой склон cliff
крышка cover, lid
кто who?; **кто говорит?** who's calling?
кто-нибудь someone, anyone
кто-то someone
кубик льда ice cube
кувшин jug
куда? where to?; **куда вы
  собираетесь?** where are you going?
кулинария deli
купальный костюм swimsuit
купание swimming
купаться to go for a swim
купе compartment *(in train)*
купюра banknote
курильщик smoker
курить smoke
курс обмена exchange rate
куртка jacket
кусать bite, sting
кусок piece; **кусочек фрукта** a piece
  of fruit
кухня kitchen
кухонное полотенце dish towel

Лл

лампа lamp
латтэ latte
левый left
лёгкий lightweight
легко it's easy
лёгкое lung
лёд ice
лезвие razor
лейкопластырь Elastoplast®, sticking
  plaster
лекарство medicine
лес forest
лесбиянка lesbian
лестница stairs
летать to fly
лето summer
линзы lenses

линия line
линия метро underground line
лист sheet, leaf
листовка leaflet
литр litre
лифт lift
лицо person, face
лоб forehead
ловить/поймать to catch
лодыжка ankle
ложка spoon
ломать/сломать to break; **сломать ногу** to break one's leg
ломтик slice
лошадь horse
луна moon
лучше better; **лучше было бы …** it's better to …
лучший best
лыжи skis
лыжный спорт skiing; **лыжная палка** ski pole; **лыжные ботинки** ski boots; **лыжный курорт** ski resort
льгота concession
льготный тариф discount fare
любимый favourite
любить to love, to like
любом: в любом случае anyway
люди people
Люксембург Luxembourg

Мм

магазин shop
мазь ointment
май May
маленький little, small
мало few, little
мама mother, mum
марка stamp
марля gauze
март march
маршрут route
масло oil, butter
масса mass
материал material

матрас mattress
матч match *(game)*
машина car
маяк lighthouse
медленно slowly
медленный slow
медовый месяц honeymoon
медсестра nurse
между between
международный international; **международный денежный перевод** international money order
мелочь small change
мельница mill
менеджер manager
менее, чем less than
меньше less
меню menu
меня зовут my name is
менять/поменять to change
мёртвый dead
местное время local time
место place, seat; **место для парковки** parking space
месяц month
месячные period *(menstrual)*
метр metre
Метро metro, underground
метрополитен metro, underground
мечеть mosque
микроволновая печь microwave
милиционер policeman, policewoman
милиция police
милый nice, dear
мимо past
минеральная вода mineral water
минимальный least
министр minister
минута minute; **минуточку!** wait a moment!
мир world, peace
миска bowl
мисс Miss
мне, меня, мной me; **мне двадцать два года** I'm 22 years old
мнение opinion

много lots, a lot (of), many
множество large quantity
мобильный телефон mobile phone
может быть maybe
мой, моя, моё my, mine
мокрый wet
моллюск shellfish
молния zip
молодёжная турбаза youth hostel
молодой young
момент moment
монастырь monastery
монета coin
мопед moped
море sea
морепродукты seafood
морозилка freezer
морская водоросль seaweed
морской курорт seaside resort
мост bridge
мотоцикл motorbike
мочалка facecloth
мочь/с-мочь to be able to; **я не могу**
 I can't
муж husband
мужской туалет gents' toilet
музей museum
музыка music
муравей ant
мусор rubbish; **выносить/вынести**
 мусор to take the rubbish out
мусорная корзина dustbin
мусорное ведро wastebin
муха fly
мы we
мыло soap
мыть to wash; **мыть/помыть**
 голову to wash one's hair
мышца muscle
мышь mouse
мясной отдел butcher's

Нн

на on, in, at, by; **на час** for an hour; **на**
машине by car; **на себя** pull

наволочка pillowcase
награда prize, award
над above
надёжный safe, reliable
надоесть to be fed up; **мне надоело**
 I'm fed up
наём hire
назад back, return
назначать цену to charge
накрывать/накрыть to cover;
 накрывать стол to lay the table
налево от to the left of
наличии: в наличии available
наличные cash; **платить**
 наличными to pay cash
налог tax
намереваться сделать что-либо
 to intend to
намеренно on purpose
напасть to attack
напиток drink
наполнять/наполнить to fill
напоминать/напомнить to remind
направление direction
направо от to the right of
напротив opposite
напуганный scared
нарезанный sliced
наркотики drugs
наружу outside
нас, нам, нами us
насекомое insect
насос bicycle pump
настоящее: в настоящее время at
 the moment
настоящий real, genuine
натуральный natural, organic
находить/найти to find
национальный public, national;
 национальный праздник national
 holiday
начало beginning; **в начале** at the
 beginning
начинать/начать to begin, to start
наш, наша, наше, наши our, ours
НДС VAT

не not; **не позже** as soon as
небо sky
небоскрёб skyscraper
невеста fiancée
негазированная вода still water
неделя week
независимый independent
незамужняя single *(woman)*
неисправность breakdown
некоторый some; **некоторые** some people
некурящий non-smoker *(m)*
некурящая non-smoker *(f)*
немедленно right away
немец German *(m)*
немецкий German *(adj)*
немка German *(f)*
немного just a little
ненавидеть to hate
необходимый necessary
неплохо it's not bad
неправильный wrong
нервный nervous
несколько several
несовременный dated, old-fashioned
несчастный случай accident
нет no; **нет, спасибо** no, thank you
неудобный uncomfortable
ни одного/ни одной not any
нигде nowhere
Нидерланды Netherlands
нижнее бельё underwear
низкий low; **низкое давление** low blood pressure
низкий short
низкокалорийный low-calorie
никогда never
никто nobody
ничего nothing
но but
новичок beginner
новость news
новый new
Новый Год new year
нога leg, foot

ноготь nail
нож knife
ножницы scissors
ноль zero
номер number
нормальный fine
нос nose
носить/нести to carry, to wear
носки socks
носовой платок handkerchief
ноутбук laptop
ночная рубашка nightdress
ночной клуб nightclub
ночь night
ноябрь November
нуждаться to need
нужно to have to; **мне нужно идти** I have to go
нужный necessary
нырять to dive

Оо

оба both
обгореть to get sunburnt
обдумывать/обдумать to think about
обед lunch
обедать to have lunch
обезболивающее anaesthetic
обещать/пообещать to promise
обжигаться/обжечься to burn oneself
облагаемый: не облагаемый налогом tax-free
обложка cover, folder
обмен exchange
обморок faint
обогреватель radiator
оборудование equipment
обратный билет return ticket
обрезаться to cut oneself
обувь shoes, footwear
общий general
объектив lens
обычно usually
огонь fire

огорчённый sorry
одежда clothes
одеться/одеться to get dressed
одеяло blanket
один one
однажды once
одноразовый disposable
одолжать to lend
ожог burn
озеро lake
океан ocean
окно window
около beside, near
окраина suburb
октябрь October
он he
она she
они they
опасный dangerous
операция operation; **перенести операцию** to have an operation
оперировать to operate
опоздать to be late; **мы опоздали на поезд** we missed the train
опрокинуть to knock down
опрятный tidy
оптик optician
опять again
организовывать to organize
оркестр orchestra
оса wasp
осень autumn
особый special
оставаться на линии hold on!
оставаться/остаться to stay
оставлять to leave behind *(object)*
останавливать/остановить to stop; **останавливаться/остановиться** to stop oneself
остановка bus/tram/trolleybus stop
остаток the rest
осторожно! watch out!
остров island
острый spicy
от from; **от себя** push
ответ answer

отвечать/ответить to answer
отдел department
отделение милиции police station
отдельно separately
отдельный separate
отдых rest, break, holiday
отдыхать/отдохнуть to rest
отец father
отказывать/отказать to refuse
открывалка bottle opener
открывать/открыть to open
открытка postcard
открытый open
откуда вы? where are you from?
отлив low tide
отличный perfect
отличный от different from
отменить to cancel
отопление heating
отправитель sender
отъезд checkout, departure
официальный праздник public holiday
официант waiter
официантка waitress
очевидный obvious
очень very
очередь queue
очки glasses
ошибка mistake; **допустить ошибку** to make a mistake

Пп

падать/упасть to fall
палатка tent
палец finger
памятник monument
панама sunhat
пара pair
парикмахер hairdresser
парк park
парк аттракционов funfair
парк отдыха theme park
парковаться/припарковаться to park

паром ferry
парус sail; **парусный спорт** sailing; **заниматься парусным спортом** to go sailing
паспорт passport
пассажир passenger
Пасха Easter
паук spider
пахнуть to smell; **хорошо/плохо пахнуть** to smell good/bad
пациент patient
певец singer *(m)*
певица singer *(f)*
пейзаж landscape, scenery
пена для бритья shaving foam
пепельница ashtray
первый first; **первый класс** first class; **первый этаж** first floor
переводить/перевести to translate; **переводить/перевести деньги** to transfer money
перед in front of
передний front; **передняя фара** headlight
перезванивать/перезвонить to call back
перелом fracture
пересадка connection
переспать с to sleep with
переходить/перейти to cross
песня song
песок sand
петь sing
печатать/напечатать to type
печень liver
печь to bake
пешеход pedestrian; **пешеходная улица** pedestrianized street
пижама pyjamas
пикник picnic; **устроить пикник** to have a picnic
ПИН код PIN (number)
пирог pie
писать to pee
писать to write; **как это пишется?** how do you spell it?

письмо letter
пить/выпить to drink
питьевая вода drinking water
пищевое отравление food poisoning
плавание swimming
плавать to swim
плавки swimming trunks
плакат poster
плакать/заплакать to cry
план plan
пластмассовый plastic
плата fare
платить/заплатить to pay
платформа platform
плед rug
плеер personal stereo, Walkman®
плёнка film
плечо shoulder
пломба filling
плоский flat
плохой bad; **плохо** it's bad
площадь square; **красная площадь** Red Square
пляж beach
пляжный зонт beach umbrella
по крайней мере at least
побережье coast, seaside; **на побережье** at the seaside
повесть novel, story
поворачивать/повернуть to turn
повреждённый damaged
повторять/повторить to repeat
погода weather; **погода плохая** the weather's bad
погружение с аквалангом scuba diving
под under, below
подарок present; **подарочная упаковка** gift wrap
подбородок chin
подгузник nappy
поддерживать общение to stay in touch
поднимать/поднять to put up, to lift, to raise
подниматься/подняться to get up

подписывать/подписать to sign
подпись signature
подросток teenager
подруга friend (f)
подтверждать/подтвердить to confirm
подушка pillow
подъёмник ski lift
поезд train; **поезд до Москвы** the train to Moscow
поездка trip
пожалуйста please, you're welcome
пожар! fire!
пожарные fire brigade
пожилые люди elderly people
позавчера the day before yesterday
позади behind, at the back of
позвать кого-нибудь to fetch someone
поздний late
пока while; **пока!** bye!
показывать/показать to show
покататься на машине to go for a drive
поклонник fan
покупать/купить to buy
пол sex, gender, floor; **на полу** on the floor
полдень noon
полезный useful
полиция police
полиэтиленовый пакет plastic bag
полкило half-kilo
пол-литра half-litre
полночь midnight
полный full, complete; **полное отключение** blackout; **полный пансион** full board; **полный тариф** full fare; **полная стоимость** full price; **на полном ходу** at full speed
половина half
поломка breakdown
полотенце towel
полтора часа an hour and a half
полупансион half-board
получать/получить to get, to receive

получить деньги назад to get a refund
полчаса half an hour
помнить to remember
помогать/помочь to help; **помогите!** help!
по-моему in my opinion
помолвлен engaged
помощь help; **звать на помощь** to call for help
понедельник Monday
понимать/понять to understand
поражать/поразить to shock
порошок powder
порт port
портить to spoil
портрет portrait
португалец Portuguese person (m)
португалка Portuguese person (f)
португальский Portuguese
порядок order; **я в порядке** I'm fine
посадка boarding
посеребрённый silver-plated
посещать/посетить to visit
посещение visit
после after
последний last: **в последний момент** at the last minute
последний last
послезавтра the day after tomorrow
посольство embassy
посуда dishes; **мыть посуду** to do the dishes
посудомоечная машина dishwasher
посылать to send
посылка parcel
пот sweat
потеряться to get lost
потом then
потому что because
поторапливайтесь! hurry up!
похмелье hangover
похожий like, similar
почему why
почка kidney
почта mail, post, post office

почтальон postman
почти almost
почтовый post; **почтовое отделение** post office; **почтовый код** postcode; **почтовый ящик** postbox
поэтому therefore
правда it's true
правильный correct
право right
правый right, correct
практический practical
прачечная launderette
пребывание stay, visit
предлагать/предложить to suggest, to offer, to propose
предложение sentence, suggestion
предпочитать to prefer
представление show, presentation, performance
предупреждать to warn
предыдущий previous
прежде всего first of all
презерватив condom
пресса press
прибытие arrival, check-in
привет! hi!
прививать против to vaccinate against
привык to be used to
приглашать/пригласить to invite
приготовленный cooked, prepared
приезд arrival
приезжать/приехать to arrive
приёмная reception room
приземляться/приземлиться to land
прикурить не найдётся? do you have a light?
прилив high tide
приложение supplement
приманка для туристов tourist trap
примерочная fitting room
примерять/ примерить to try on
принести что-нибудь to fetch something

принимать ванну to take a bath
принимать/принять to accept, to take; **принимать/принять душ** to take a shower
приносить/принести to bring
приправа dressing
природа nature
присматривать/присмотреть to look after
приходить/прийти to come
причал quay
приятного аппетита enjoy your meal!
пробка bath plug
пробка fuse, traffic jam
проблема problem
пробовать/попробовать to try, to taste
проверять/проверить to check
проводить/провести to spend
прогноз forecast
прогноз погоды weather forecast
проголодаться to be hungry
программа programme
прогулка walk
прогулочная коляска pushchair
продавать to sell
продавец shop assistant; **продавец газет** newsagent
продаётся sale, for sale; **в продаже** in the sale
продукт product
прозрачная лампочка light bulb
произведение искусства work of art
прокат rental, hire
прокладка sanitary towel
пропуск pass
пропустить to miss
проспект leaflet, prospectus
проспект avenue
простите? excuse me?
простуда cold; **простудиться** to have a cold
просьба не беспокоить do not disturb

протекать to leak
против against
противозачаточное средство contraceptive
противоположность opposite
профессия profession
прохладный cool
проходить to pass
процент percent
прошлый last; **в прошлом году** last year
прыщик spot
прямо straight ahead, straight on
прямой straight, right
прямой direct
птица bird
пудра powder
пункт point
пурпурный purple
пускать to let
пустой empty
путеводитель guidebook
путешествие journey
путешествовать to travel
путь way
пчела bee
пьеса play
пьяный drunk
пятница Friday
пятно stain

Рр

работа job, work; **работа по дому** housework
работать to work
рад(а) познакомиться pleased to meet you!
радиатор radiator
радио radio
радиостанция radio station
раз once, time; **три/четыре раза** three/four times; **раз в день/раз в час** once an hour
развалины ruins; **в развалинах** in ruins

разворот U-turn
раздетый naked
разливное пиво draught beer
разменивать/разменять to change
размер size
разница во времени time difference
разражаться to burst
разрешать to let, to allow
район area, district
ракетка racket
рана wound
рано early
раньше before, earlier
расист racist
расписание timetable
распродажа sales
расставаться/расстаться to split up, to part
расстояние distance; **на расстоянии 10 километров** 10 kilometres away
расстроенный upset
расстройство желудка diarrhoea
растение plant
расти/вырасти to grow
расчёска comb
рациональный reasonable
рвота to vomit
ребёнок baby, child
ребро rib
ревматизм rheumatism
регистрационный номер registration number
регистрация check-in
регистрироваться/зарегистрироваться to check in
редкий rare, unusual
редко seldom, rarely
резать to cut
рейс flight
река river
рекомендовать to recommend
ремень безопасности safety belt
рентген X-rays
ресепшн reception

ресторан restaurant; **ресторан быстрого обслуживания** fast-food restaurant
рецепт prescription
риск risk
родители parents
розовое вино rosé wine
розовый pink
рок rock
роликовые коньки rollerblades
роскошный luxurious
роскошь luxury
рот mouth
рубашка shirt
рука arm, hand
рукав sleeve
ручка pen
ручной hand; **ручная кладь** hand luggage; **ручной работы** hand-made; **ручной тормоз** handbrake
рыба fish
рыбный fish; **рыбный магазин** fish shop; **рыбный отдел** fish counter
рыжий red
рынок market
рюкзак backpack, rucksack
рядом с right beside

Сс

с with; **с тех пор (как)** since
CD диск CD
сад garden
садиться/сесть to sit down
сайт website
салфетка napkin
сам himself
самокат scooter
самолет plane
самом: на самом деле in fact
сандалии sandals
сантиметр centimetre
сбить to knock down
сбор toll
свет light
светло-голубой light blue

свеча candle
свеча зажигания spark plug
свидание appointment; **назначать/ назначить свидание** to make an appointment
свитер sweater
свой/своя/своё/свои own
связываться to get in touch
связываться/связаться to contact
связь connection, link
сдача change
себя oneself
север north
сегодня today; **сегодня вечером** tonight, this evening
сейчас now
секретарь на ресепшн receptionist
сельская местность countryside
семья family
сенная лихорадка hay fever
сентябрь September
сердечный приступ heart attack
сердце heart
серебряный silver
середина middle
серёжки earrings
сёрфинг surfing
серый grey
серьёзный serious
сестра sister
сигара cigar
сигарета cigarette
сигаретная бумага cigarette paper
сигнал signal
сильный strong
синагога synagogue
синий blue
сироп syrup
скала rock, cliff
скалолазание climbing
скандальный shocking
скидка discount; **сделать скидку** to give a discount
сковородка frying pan
сколько? how much/many?; **сколько это стоит?** how much does it cost?;

сколько вам/тебе лет? how old are you?; **сколько раз?** how many times?

скорая помощь ambulance

скорее rather

скоро soon

скорость speed

скотч whisky, sellotape®

слабый weak

сладкий sweet

слайд slide

следующий next

слепой blind

слишком too; **слишком плохо** too bad; **слишком много** too many, too much

сложный difficult, complicated

сломанный broken

сломаться to break down

случай: в случае in case

случайно by chance, by accident

случаться/случиться to happen

слушать to listen

слышать/услышать to hear

смеяться to laugh

смириться с to put up with

смотреть to watch; **смотреть на** to look at

снаружи outside

снег snow

снимать to hire

снимать/снять to withdraw

снимок photograph

снова again

снотворное sleeping pill

собирать to pack; collect; **собирать чемодан** to pack one's suitcase

собор cathedral

собрание meeting

совет advice; **просить совета** to ask someone's advice

советовать/посоветовать to advise

современный modern

совсем нет not at all

Соединённые Штаты United States

сок juice

сокращать to reduce

солёный salty

солнечный sun; **солнечные очки** sunglasses; **солнечный удар** sunstroke

солнце sun

соль salt

сон sleep

сообщение message

сопровождать/сопроводить to go with, to accompany

сосед neighbour (m)

соседка neighbour (f)

спальный мешок sleeping bag

спасать to save

спасибо thanks; **спасибо вам** thank you; **большое вам спасибо** thank you very much; **спасибо** thanks to

спать to sleep

спелый ripe

специя spice

спираль coil (contraceptive)

спичка match (for fire)

спокойной ночи goodnight

спорт sport

спортивный sporty

спортплощадка sports ground

справляться to manage

справочная directory enquiries

справочник directory

спрашивать/спросить to ask

спущенная шина flat tyre

среда Wednesday

среди among

средний medium

средняя школа secondary school

средство от насекомых insecticide

срок годности, срок действия expiry date

срочность emergency; **в срочном порядке** in an emergency

срочный urgent

стадион stadium

стакан glass

станция station

станция метро underground station

старый old; **старый город** old town

степень degree
стиль style
стиральный washing; **стиральная машина** washing machine; **стиральный порошок** washing powder
стирать/постирать to do the washing
стирка washing
стихийное бедствие disaster
стоимость charge, cost
стоить cost
стол table
столовая ложка tablespoon
стоматолог dentist
сторона side
стоять в очереди to queue
страдать to suffer
страна country
странный strange
страховка insurance
строить/построить to build
студент student *(m)*
студентка student *(f)*
стукнуться to bump
стул chair
ступня foot
стыд shame
стыдно it's a shame
суббота Saturday
субтитрами: с субтитрами subtitled
сувенир souvenir
судно boat
сумка bag
супермаркет supermarket
сухой dry
сушить/высушить to dry
сфотографировать что-либо/кого-либо to take a photo of something/someone
сходить/сойти to get off
сцепление clutch
счастливого пути! have a good trip!
счастливый happy
счёт bill
счётчик meter

считать to count
сын son
сырой raw
сэконд-хэнд second-hand
сюрприз surprise

Тт

табак tobacco
табачный киоск tobacconist's
таблетка tablet
таз washbasin
так so
также also
такой же same
такси taxi
таксист taxi driver
талия waist
там there
таможня customs
тампон tampon
танец dance
танцевать to dance
таракан cockroach
тарелка plate
тариф fare
твой your, yours
те those
театр theatre
телевизор television
телефон phone
телефонист switchboard operator *(m)*
телефонистка switchboard operator *(f)*
телефонный phone; **телефонная кабинка** phone box; **телефонная карта** phonecard; **телефонный код** dialling code; **телефонный номер** phone number
тело body
тем лучше all the better
тем не менее although
тёмный dark
температура fever, temperature; **мерить/померить температуру** to take one's temperature

теннис tennis; **теннисные туфли** tennis shoes; **теннисный корт** tennis court

тень shade

тёплый warm

терапевт GP

термос Thermos® flask

терраса terrace

терять/потерять to lose

тётя aunt

течение: в течение during

течь to leak, to flow

тип type

типичный typical

тихий quiet

то же самое same

товары goods

тогда then

тоже also

толкать push

только only, just; **только один** just one; **я только приехал** I've just arrived

тонуть to drown

торговый центр shopping centre

тормоз brake

тормозить to brake

торопиться to hurry

тот that one

тошнить to feel sick; **меня тошнит** I feel sick

трава grass

травмированный injured

традиционный traditional

трамвай tram

транспорт traffic

тратить/потратить to waste

троллейбус trolleybus

тропинка path

труба chimney

трудный hard, difficult

трусы underpants

туалет toilet

туалетная бумага toilet paper

туалетные принадлежности toiletries

тур package holiday

турбюро travel agency

туризм tourism

турист tourist *(m)*

туристка tourist *(f)*

туристическая обувь walking boots

ты you

тяжёлый heavy

тянуть to pull

Уу

убивать/убить to kill

убирать/убрать to clean up

уверенный sure, certain

увлажнитель moisturizer

удалять/удалить to remove

удача luck

удивлять/удивить to surprise

удобный comfortable

удовольствие pleasure

удостоверение личности proof of identity

уезжать/уехать to leave, to go away

ужасный terrible

уже already

ужин dinner

ужинать to have dinner

узкий tight

узнавать/узнать to recognize

узнать to learn, to find out

указатель indicator

укачивать to be seasick; **меня укачивает** I'm seasick

укол injection

укус bite, sting

улица street

улучшиться to get better

улыбаться/улыбнуться to smile

улыбка smile

умереть to die

уметь to know how to

универмаг department store

упакованный packed

упаковка packet, parcel

ура! hurray!, cheers!

услуга favour; **оказать кому-нибудь услугу** to do someone a favour
уставший tired
устаревший out of date, old
утверждение statement
утка duck
утомлённый exhausted
утомлять to exhaust, to tire out
утро morning
утюг iron
ухо ear
ухудшиться to get worse
учить/выучить to learn
ушные тампоны earplugs
Уэльс Wales
уэльский Welsh

Фф

факс fax
факт fact
фамилия surname
фанат fan
февраль February
фейерверк fireworks
фен hairdryer
фестиваль festival
фильм film, movie
фляга flask
фольга tinfoil
фонарь torch
форма shape, uniform
фотоаппарат camera
фотография photograph
Франция France
французский French
фунт pound
фургон caravan
футбол soccer

Хх

хватит: этого хватит that's enough
химчистка dry cleaner's
хирургический спирт surgical spirit
хлеб bread

хлопок cotton
ходить в походы to go hiking
ходить по магазинам to go shopping
холм hill
холодильник fridge
холодный cold; **холодно** it's cold
холостой single (man)
хороший good
хорошо good, well; **у меня всё хорошо** I'm very well; **хорошо приготовленный** well done (meat)
хорошо проводить/провести время to enjoy oneself
хотеть to want; **я бы хотел** I'd like; **хотеть пить** to be thirsty; **хотеть спать** to be sleepy
хотя although
храм temple, church
хранить/сохранить to keep
хрупкий fragile
художник artist
худой thin
хуже worse; **это хуже, чем ...** it's worse than ...

Цц

цвет colour
целый whole; **целый день** all day
цена price
центр centre; **центр города** town centre
церковь church
цирк circus
цифровой фотоаппарат digital camera

Чч

чаевые tip
чайная ложка teaspoon
час hour
часовня chapel
частный private
часто often
часть part; **быть частью** to be a part of

часы watch
чаша bowl
чашка cup
чей/чья/чьё whose
чек cheque, receipt
человек person, man
чемодан suitcase
через across
через час in an hour
чёрный c black
честный honest
четверг Thursday
четверть quarter; **четверть одиннадцатого** a quarter past ten; **четверть часа** a quarter of an hour
чинить to repair
число date
чистый clean, tidy
читать/прочитать to read
член member
что what; **что вы хотите?** what do you want?
что-нибудь anything, something
что-то something; **что-то ещё** something else
чувствительный sensitive
чувство sense, feeling
чувствовать to feel; **хорошо/плохо себя чувствовать** to feel good/bad
чудесный wonderful

Шш

шаг step
шампунь shampoo
шапка hat
шарик scoop; **два шарика мороженого** two scoops of ice cream
шерсть wool
шествие procession
шея neck
шина tyre
широкий wide
шлёпки flip-flops
шорты shorts
шотландец Scotsman

шотландка Scotswoman
Шотландия Scotland
шотландский Scottish
шоу show
штопор bottle opener, corkscrew
штраф fine
шум noise
шуметь to make a noise
шумный noisy
щётка brush

Ээ

эконом класс economy class
экскурсионное бюро tourist office
экскурсия guided tour
экскурсовод tour guide
экспресс express
электрический electric
электричество electricity
электробритва electric shaver
электронная почта e-mail
электронный адрес e-mail address
эпилептический epileptic
эспрессо espresso
этаж storey
эти these
это it is, they are; **это зависит от** it depends on; **это неважно** it doesn't matter

Юю

юбилей anniversary
юбка skirt
ювелирные изделия jewellery
ювелирный jewellery; **ювелирный магазин** jeweller's
юг south

Яя

я I
язык language, tongue
январь January
ярмарка fair

GRAMMAR

NOUNS There are no words in Russian for *the* and *a*. The context will tell you whether a noun is definite or indefinite.

There are **three genders** in Russian: masculine, feminine and neuter. You can tell the gender of a noun by looking at its ending. Exceptions are the few nouns ending in **-ь**: you have to learn whether these are masculine or feminine.

Masculine nouns end with a consonant, an **-й** or a **-ь**.
    парк (park)   трамвай (tram)   Кремль (Kremlin)

Feminine nouns end in **-а**, **-я**, **-ия** or **-ь**.
    школа (school)   неделя (week)   экскурсия (excursion)
    дочь (daughter)

Neuter nouns end in **-о**, **-е** or **-ие**.
    метро (metro)   море (sea)   здание (building)

A few nouns ending in **-а** or **-я** are masculine because of their meaning.
    мужчина (man)   папа (dad)   дядя (uncle)

There are a very few nouns ending in **-мя** which are neuter.
    время (time)

Some nouns exist only in the plural, eg **деньги** (money). These are shown in the dictionary section by (*pl*).

Most masculine nouns have their plural in **-ы** or **-и**.
    ресторан (restaurant) **→** рестораны
    киоск (kiosk) **→** киоски
    рубль (rouble) **→** рубли
    музей (museum) **→** музеи

A few masculine nouns have their plural in **-а**.
    дом (house) **→** дома

город (town) ➔ города
поезд (train) ➔ поезда

Feminine nouns have their plural in **-ы** or **-и**.
гостиница (hotel) ➔ гостиницы
библиотека (library) ➔ библиотеки
площадь (square) ➔ площади

Neuter nouns ending in **-о** generally have their plural in **-а**.
пятно (spot) ➔ пятна

Common exceptions are:
ухо (ear) ➔ уши
яблоко (apple) ➔ яблоки

Neuter nouns ending in **-е** generally have their plural in **-я**.
море (sea) ➔ моря

Neuter nouns ending in **-мя** have their plural in **-ена**.
имя (name) ➔ имена

Some common nouns have an irregular plural form and occasionally use a different word altogether.
брат (brother) ➔ братья
муж (husband) ➔ мужья
стул (chair) ➔ стулья
друг (friend) ➔ друзья
сын (son) → сыновья
дочь (daughter) ➔ дочери
мать (mother) ➔ матери
человек (person) ➔ люди
ребёнок (child) ➔ дети

All nouns decline, using a different form depending on their function in the phrase. There are six cases in Russian.

The **nominative** is the case used for the subject of the verb.
телефон не работает <u>the telephone</u> isn't working

The **accusative** is used for the direct object.
я хочу купить карту. I want to buy <u>a map</u>

It is also used after the prepositions **в** and **на** (to/into/onto) when expressing motion or direction.

> **я иду на почту** I'm going to <u>the post office</u>

The **genitive** is used for possession.

> **адрес гостиницы** the address of <u>the hotel</u>

It is also used after certain prepositions, eg **около** (around), **без** (without), **из** (from, out of), **с** (from), **для** (for), **от** (away from), **до** (up to), **после** (after).

The **dative** is used for indirect objects.

> **я хочу позвонить сестре** I want to call <u>my sister</u>

The **instrumental** is used to show how, by whom or with what an action is performed.

> **я приехал автобусом** I came by <u>bus</u>
> **надо платить рублями** you need to pay with <u>roubles</u>

It is also used after certain prepositions, eg **с** (with), **между** (between), **над** (above), **под** (beneath), **перед** (in front of) and **за** (behind).
я иду с вами I'm coming with <u>you</u>

The **prepositional** case is always preceded by a preposition, commonly **в** (in), **на** (on) and **о** (about).

> **он на поезде** he's on <u>the train</u>
> **мы говорили о театре** we talked about <u>the theatre</u>

Table of regular noun declensions

• Masculine nouns
eg **билет** (ticket), **словарь** (dictionary), **музей** (museum)

Singular

Nom.	билет	словарь	музей
Acc.	билет	словарь	музей
Gen.	билета	словаря	музея
Dat.	билету	словарю	музею
Inst.	билетом	словарём	музеем
Prep.	о билете	о словаре	о музее

Plural

Nom.	билеты	словари	музеи
Acc.	билеты	словари	музеи
Gen.	билетов	словарей	музеев
Dat.	билетам	словарям	музеям
Inst.	билетами	словарями	музеями
Prep.	о билетах	о словарях	о музеях

• Feminine nouns

eg **газета** (newspaper), **неделя** (week), **фамилия** (surname), **площадь** (square)

Singular

Nom.	газета	неделя	фамилия	площадь
Acc.	газету	неделю	фамилию	площадь
Gen.	газеты	недели	фамилии	площади
Dat.	газете	неделе	фамилии	площади
Inst.	газетой	неделей	фамилией	площадью
Prep.	о газете	о неделе	о фамилии	о площади

Plural

Nom.	газеты	недели	фамилии	площади
Acc.	газеты	недели	фамилии	площади
Gen.	газет	недель	фамилий	площадей
Dat.	газетам	неделям	фамилиям	площадям
Inst.	газетами	неделями	фамилиями	площадями
Prep.	о газетах	о неделях	о фамилиях	о площадях

• Neuter nouns

eg **дело** (business, matter), **здание** (building), **имя** (name)

Singular

Nom.	дело	здание	имя
Acc.	дело	здание	имя
Gen.	дела	здания	имени
Dat.	делу	зданию	имени
Inst.	делом	зданием	именем
Prep.	о деле	о здании	об имени

Plural

Nom.	дела	здания	имена
Acc.	дела	здания	имена
Gen.	дел	зданий	имён
Dat.	делам	зданиям	именам
Inst.	делами	зданиями	именами
Prep.	о делах	о зданиях	об именах

Most nouns of foreign origin do not decline, eg **кино** (cinema), **метро** (metro), **такси** (taxi), **кофе** (coffee), **кафе** (café), **меню** (menu).

Like nouns, **PERSONAL PRONOUNS** decline. Note that there are two words for "you" in Russian: **ты** is used when you are addressing one person with whom you are on informal terms; **вы** is used when you are addressing more than one person, or one person with whom you are on formal terms.

	I	you	he	she	it	we	you	they
Nom.	я	ты	он	она	оно	мы	вы	они
Acc.	меня	тебя	его	её	его	нас	вас	их
Gen.	меня	тебя	его	её	его	нас	вас	их
Dat.	мне	тебе	ему	ей	ему	нам	вам	им
Inst.	мной	тобой	им	ей	им	нами	вами	ими
Prep.	обо мне	о тебе	о нём	о ней	о нём	о нас	о вас	о них

The pronouns and demonstrative adjectives "this" and "that" also decline, agreeing with the noun to which they refer.

	Masculine	*Feminine*	*Neuter*	*Plural*
This	этот	эта	это	эти
That	тот	та	то	те

After the number 1 and any number ending in 1 (21, 31 etc, except 11), the following noun appears in the nominative singular.

21 год (21 years)
101 рубль (101 roubles)
91 километр (91 kilometres)

After the numbers 2, 3, 4 and any number ending in 2, 3, 4 (except 12, 13, 14), the following noun appears in the genitive singular.

22 года (22 years)
54 рубля (54 roubles)

GRAMMAR

After the numbers 5 to 20 and any numbers ending in 5, 6, 7, 8, 9 or 0 thereafter, the following noun appears in the genitive plural.

16 лет (16 years)
28 километров (28 kilometres)
100 рублей (100 roubles)

Like nouns, **ADJECTIVES** decline, agreeing in gender, number and case with the noun to which they refer, eg **интересная экскурсия** (interesting excursion).

NB Adjective endings in **-ого** or **-его** pronounce the "r" as a "v".

новый (new)

	Masculine	Feminine	Neuter	Plural
Nom.	новый	новая	новое	новые
Acc.	новый	новую	новое	новые
Gen.	нового	новой	нового	новых
Dat.	новому	новой	новому	новым
Inst.	новым	новой	новым	новыми
Prep.	новом	новой	новом	новых

русский (Russian)

	Masculine	Feminine	Neuter	Plural
Nom.	русский	русская	русское	русские
Acc.	русский	русскую	русское	русские
Gen.	русского	русской	русского	русских
Dat.	русскому	русской	русскому	русским
Inst.	русским	русской	русским	русскими
Prep.	русском	русской	русском	русских

последний (last)

	Masculine	Feminine	Neuter	Plural
Nom.	последний	последняя	последнее	последние
Acc.	последний	последнюю	последнее	последние
Gen.	последнего	последней	последнего	последних
Dat.	последнему	последней	последнему	последним
Inst.	последним	последней	последним	последними
Prep.	последнем	последней	последнем	последних

ORDINAL NUMBERS agree in gender, number and case with the noun to which they refer and decline as adjectives:

	Masculine	*Feminine*	*Neuter*	*Plural*
first	первый	первая	первое	первые

POSSESSIVE ADJECTIVES agree in gender, number and case with the noun to which they refer, except for **его/её/их** (his/her/their) which do not change.

это мой билет this is my ticket

	Masculine	*Feminine*	*Neuter*	*Plural*
my/mine	мой	моя	моё	мои
your/yours	твой	твоя	твоё	твои
his	его	его	его	его
her/hers	её	её	её	её
our/ours	наш	наша	наше	наши
your/yours	ваш	ваша	ваше	ваши
their/theirs	их	их	их	их

Adverbs are generally formed by replacing the masculine adjective ending **-ый**, **-ой**, **-ий** by **-о**, eg

хороший (good) → хорошо (well)
быстрый (quick) → быстро (quickly)

The comparative is generally formed by placing **более** (more) or **менее** (less) in front of the adjective, eg **более интересный** (more interesting), **менее интересный** (less interesting).

There are some frequently used comparatives that are irregular:

дешёвый (cheap) → дешевле (cheaper)
дорогой (expensive) → дороже (more expensive)
большой (big) → больше (bigger)
маленький (small) → меньше (smaller)
хороший (good) → лучше (better)
плохой (bad) → хуже (worse)
высокий (tall) → выше (taller)
низкий (low) → ниже (lower)
старый (old) → старше (older)
молодой (young) → моложе (younger)

A comparative phrase is formed by the word **чем** (than):

> **эта гостиница дороже, чем та** this hotel is more expensive than that one

The superlative is usually formed by placing **самый** (most) in front of the adjective

> **дешёвый** (cheap) → **самый дешёвый** (cheapest)

VERBS in Russian generally have two forms, corresponding to **two different aspects**.

All verbs in this book are shown in both aspects: first the imperfective and then the perfective, eg **читать/прочитать** to read

The **imperfective** aspect is used for actions which are repeated or continuous. It can be used in present, past and future forms.

> **я читаю газету** I am reading the newspaper
> **я читал газету** I was reading the newspaper
> **я буду читать газету** I will be reading the newspaper

The **perfective** aspect is used for actions which happen only once, are complete or are limited in time. It can be used in past and future forms only.

> **я прочитал газету** I finished reading the newspaper
> **я прочитаю газету** I will finish reading the newspaper

To work out what endings to put on the different forms of Russian verbs, you need to be aware that they fall broadly into **two conjugations** or groups.

The most typical verbs of the **first conjugation** have an infinitive ending in **-ать** or **-ять**.

	читать (to read)
я	чита-**ю**
ты	чита-**ешь**
он/она	чита-**ет**
мы	чита-**ем**
вы	чита-**ете**
они	чита-**ют**

Below are a few common first-conjugation verbs which do not follow the typical pattern:

	ждать (to wait)		жить (to live)
я	жд-**у**	я	жив-**у**
ты	жд-**ёшь**	ты	жив-**ёшь**
он/она	жд-**ёт**	он/она	жив-**ёт**
мы	жд-**ём**	мы	жив-**ём**
вы	жд-**ёте**	вы	жив-**ёте**
они	жд-**ут**	они	жив-**ут**

	мочь (to be able)		идти (to go on foot)
я	мог-**у**	я	ид-**у**
ты	мож-**ешь**	ты	ид-**ёшь**
он/она	мож-**ет**	он/она	ид-**ёт**
мы	мож-**ем**	мы	ид-**ём**
вы	мож-**ете**	вы	ид-**ёте**
они	мог-**ут**	они	ид-**ут**

Verbs of the **second conjugation** commonly have an infinitive ending in **-ить**.

	говорить (to speak)
я	говор-**ю**
ты	говор-**ишь**
он/она	говор-**ит**
мы	говор-**им**
вы	говор-**ите**
они	говор-**ят**

Some second conjugation verbs change the last consonant of the stem or slip a letter **л** between the stem and the ending in the first person singular (**я**) form.

	ответить (to reply)		любить (to love)
я	отвеч-**у**	я	любл-**ю**
ты	ответ-**ишь**	ты	люб-**ишь**
он/она	ответ-**ит**	он/она	люб-**ит**
мы	ответ-**им**	мы	люб-**им**
вы	ответ-**ите**	вы	люб-**ите**
они	ответ-**ят**	они	люб-**ят**

Below are two common irregular verbs:

	хотеть (to want)		есть (to eat)
я	хоч-**у**	я	ем
ты	хоч-**ешь**	ты	ешь
он/она	хоч-**ет**	он/она	ест
мы	хот-**им**	мы	ед-**им**
вы	хот-**ите**	вы	ед-**ите**
они	хот-**ят**	они	ед-**ят**

The verb **быть** (to be) does not occur in the present tense.
я турист I'm a tourist

In the future tense, the verb **быть** (to be) conjugates as below:

я	буд-**у**
ты	буд-**ешь**
он/она	буд-**ет**
мы	буд-**ем**
вы	буд-**ете**
они	буд-**ут**

To express the verb "to have" use the preposition **у** followed by the noun or pronoun in the genitive of the person possessing the item. This is followed by **есть** and the item itself in the nominative, eg
    у меня есть паспорт I have a passport

The interrogative form is as follows:
    у вас есть билет? do you have a ticket?

The **past tense** is formed by removing the infinitive ending **-ть** of a verb with **-л** (masculine), **-ла** (feminine), **-ло** (neuter), **-ли** (plural).
    я была в Москве I was in Moscow (feminine)
    мы были в Новгороде we were in Novgorod
    он был в Иркутске? was he in Irkutsk?

The past tense of the verb **идти** (to go on foot) is irregular.
    он шёл he was going
    она шла she was going
    они шли they were going

The **future imperfective** is formed with the future of the verb **быть** (to be) followed by the imperfective infinitive.

> **каждый день я буду писать открытки** I'll write postcards every day

The **future perfective** is formed by conjugating the perfective infinitive. This often (but not always) means putting a prefix (**по-**, **про-**, **на-**, **с-**, **вы-**) in front of the imperfective infinitive.

> **я пишу открытку** I'm writing a postcard
> **я напишу открытку** I will write a postcard

The **negative** is formed by inserting **не** between the subject and the verb.

> **я не понимаю** I don't understand

Questions are usually formed simply by intonation, which rises on the most important question word of the phrase.

> **вы хотите кофе?** would you like coffee?

There are many **impersonal expressions** in Russian which use the dative case to express a state of being or necessity.

> **мне жарко** I'm hot
> **ему холодно** he's cold
> **ей плохо** he's feeling bad
> **тебе нужно** you need to
> **мне хочется есть/пить** I'm hungry/thirsty

HOLIDAYS AND FESTIVALS

NATIONAL HOLIDAYS

Here is a list of public holidays in Russia, known as **официальные праздники** *(afitsyal'nyye prazniki)*. Note that if the holiday falls on a Thursday, the Friday and Saturday are also holidays, but people will work on the Sunday. If the holiday falls on a Sunday, the Monday will also be a holiday.

1–2 January: **Новый Год** *(novy got)* **New Year**. This is a time for seeing family and eating and drinking more than usual. On 1 January, children receive presents from "Grandpa Frost", **Дед Мороз** *(dyet maros)*.

7 January: **Рождество Христово** *(razhdistvo hristova)* **Christmas**. The Russians celebrate Christmas on this date two weeks later than us because the Russian Orthodox calendar is 13 days behind.

23 February: **День защитника Отечества** *(dyen' zaschitnika atyechistva)* **Protector of Motherland Day**. This holiday was established under the Soviet regime as Soviet Army Day, and has become a kind of "men's day". People get together for meals and drinks and men receive presents.

8 March: **Международный женский день** *(mizhdoonarodny zhenski dyen')* **International Women's Day**. This was an important celebration under the Soviet regime, and is still popular today. It's the custom for men to give women flowers and presents.

1–2 May: **День весны и труда** *(dyen' visny i trooda)* **Spring and Labour Day**. Until recently it was officially termed International Workers' Solidarity Day. Now many people spend the holiday at dachas (country houses) while some attend customary demonstrations.

9 May: **День победы** *(dyen' pabyedy)* **Victory Day**. A celebration of the victory over Germany in World War II. Veterans gather in uniform, fireworks are set off and graves are decorated with flowers in memory of those who lost their lives.

12 June: **День независимости России** *(dyen' nyezavisimasti Rasii)* **Russian Independence Day**. The anniversary of Russia's Declaration of Sovereignty after the fall of the Soviet Union.

4 November: **День национального единства** *(dyen' natsyanal'nava idinstva)* **Day of National Unity**. This is the newest Russian holiday, introduced in 2005 and replacing the former national holiday on 7 November called the Day of Reconciliation.

FESTIVALS AND CELEBRATIONS

After the fall of the Soviet Union, many Soviet festivals disappeared while old religious festivals – such as 19 January **Крещение** *(krishyenii)* **Epiphany** – were revived, as were festivals commemorating certain professions (such as 7 May **Day of Radio**, 5 October **Teacher's Day**, 10 November **Day of the Police**).

13 January:	**Старый Новый год** *(stary novy got)* **Former New Year**. Still celebrated in accordance with the old Gregorian calendar.
25 January:	**Татьянин день** *(tatyanin dyen')* **Tatyana's Day (Students Day)**. Anniversary of the foundation of Moscow University and a day of celebration for all students.
March:	**Масленица** *(maslinitsa)*, the equivalent of Mardi Gras or Shrove Tuesday. The beginning of spring is celebrated with public events and special meals where blinis are usually served.
March – April:	**Пасха** *(pasHa)* **Easter**. This is the most important festival in the Orthodox church calendar, but has only been officially celebrated in recent years. The date of Easter Sunday changes every year (two weeks after Easter in the Christian Church). Russians celebrate with a cheesecake called *pasHa* and a traditional Easter cake known as *koolich*, and give each other painted Easter eggs.
1 April:	**День смеха** *(dyen' smyeHa)* **April Fool's Day (Day of Laughter)**. People play tricks on each other and newspapers publish funny stories and jokes.
12 April:	**День космонавтики** *(dyen' kasmanaftiki)* **Astronauts' Day**.
late June – late July:	The famous Saint Petersburg White Nights festival. The city's residents fill the streets and party until dawn.
1 September:	**День знаний** *(dyen' znani)*, **Day of Knowledge**. Children go back to school after the summer break with flowers, but there are no real lessons.
first weekend of September:	**День города Москвы** *(dyen' gorada maskvy)* **Moscow Festival**. Various concerts are held in the capital.
25 December:	Catholic Christmas.

USEFUL ADDRESSES

Russian National Tourist Office
E-mail: http://www.visitrussia.org.uk/

In the UK

Russian Embassy, London
6/7 Kensington Palace Gardens, London, W8 4QP, UK
Tel.: 0207 2292666
Fax: 0207 2295804
E-mail: office@rusemblon.org

In the US

Russian Embassy, Washington DC
2650 Wisconsin Ave. NW, Washington DC, 20007
Tel.: (202) 298 5700
Fax: (202) 298 5735

In Russia

British Embassy, Moscow
121099 Moscow, 10 Smolenskaya Naberezhnaya
Tel.:   00 7 495 956 7200
Fax: 00 7 495 956 7201
E-mail: moscow@britishembassy.ru

British Consulate General, Saint Petersburg
91124 St Petersburg, Pl. Proletarskoy Diktatury, 5
Tel.: 007 812 320 3200
Fax: 007 812 320 3211
E-mail: bcgspb@peterlink.ru

US Embassy, Moscow
Moscow 121099, Bolshoy Deviatinsky Pereulok No. 8
Tel: +7 (495) 728-5000
Fax: 728-5090
E-mail: consulmo@state.gov

US Consulate General, Saint Petersburg
St. Petersburg 191028, Ulitsa Furshtadskaya, 15
Tel: +7 (812) 331-2600
Fax: 331-2852
E-mail:acsstpete@state.gov

Emergency numbers:
Fire brigade: **01**
Police: **02**
Ambulance: **03**

CONVERSION TABLES

MEASUREMENTS
Only the metric system is used in Russia.

Length
1 cm ≈ 0.4 inches
30 cm ≈ 1 foot

Distance
1 metre ≈ 1 yard
1 km ≈ 0.6 miles

To convert kilometres into miles, divide by 8 and then multiply by 5.

kilometres	1	2	5	10	20	100
miles	0.6	1.25	3.1	6.25	12.50	62.50

To convert miles into kilometres, divide by 5 and then multiply by 8.

miles	1	2	5	10	20	100
kilometres	1.6	3.2	8	16	32	160

Weight
25g ≈ 1 oz   1 kg ≈ 2 lb   6 kg ≈ 1 stone

To convert kilos into pounds, divide by 5 and then multiply by 11.
To convert pounds into kilos, multiply by 5 and then divide by 11.

kilos	1	2	10	20	60	80
pounds	2.2	4.4	22	44	132	176

Liquid
1 litre ≈ 2 pints
4.5 litres ≈ 1 gallon

Temperature

To convert temperatures in Fahrenheit into Celsius, subtract 32, multiply by 5 and then divide by 9.

To convert temperatures in Celsius into Fahrenheit, divide by 5, multiply by 9 and then add 32.

Fahrenheit (°F)	32	40	50	59	68	86	100
Celsius (°C)	0	4	10	15	20	30	38

Clothes sizes

Sometimes you will find sizes given using the English-language abbreviations **XS** (Extra Small), **S** (Small), **M** (Medium), **L** (Large) and **XL** (Extra Large).

• Women's clothes

Russia	42	44	46	48	50	etc
UK	8	10	12	14	16	

• Bras (cup sizes are the same)

Russia	70	75	80	85	90	etc
UK	32	34	36	38	40	

• Men's shirts (collar size)

Russia	36	38	41	43	etc
UK	14	15	16	17	

• Men's clothes

Russia	40	42	44	46	48	50	etc
UK	30	32	34	36	38	40	

Shoe sizes

• Women's shoes

Russia	37	38	39	40	41	etc
UK	4	5	6	7	8	

• Men's shoes

Russia	40	41	42	43	44	etc
UK	7	8	9	10	11	